NEW PLAINS REVIEW
FALL 2013

I0553691

Editors and Staff

❖

Executive Editor	*Shay Rahm*
Production Chief	*Michelle Waggoner*
Editor-in-Chief	*Regan Markley*
Managing Editors	*Rhiannon James*
	Christina Morel
Poetry Editor	*Kaylee Kain*
Assistant Poetry Editors	*Taylor Verkler*
	Haley Rapacz
	Nhu Nguyen
Fiction Editor	*Maggie McGee*
Assistant Fiction Editors	*Alex Hartgrove*
	Cherie Poertner
	Aisha Alshehry
Nonfiction Editor	*J. Chance Gibbs*
Assistant Nonfiction Editors	*Ngoc Nguyen*
	Yihwa Kim
	Sarah Ventris
Special Section Editor	*Christina Morel*
Webmaster	*William Andrews*

❖

New Plains Review Publishing Group
University of Central Oklahoma
Edmond, Oklahoma

New Plains Review
ISBN-10: 0983735743
ISBN-13: 978-0-9837357-4-8

New Plains Review is a literary journal published each academic semester, sponsored by the English Department, College of Liberal Arts, at the University of Central Oklahoma. The image found on every cover of *New Plains Review* issue since 2000 is based on a painting titled "Phantom Warriors" by acclaimed Native American artist and UCO alumnus Sherman Chaddlesone.

New Plains Review
English Department, Box 184
University of Central Oklahoma
100 North University Drive
Edmond, Oklahoma 73034

(405) 974-5613
newplainsreview@gmail.com
www.libarts.uco.edu/english/newplains

Submission Information: *New Plains Review* accepts original work in prose, poetry, drama, fiction, art, and photography. Submissions are accepted by email. For editorial guidelines, please visit the website.

Ordering Information: Pricing for subscriptions, current and back issues are available through the website.

Cover Art:
Brian Forrest
Berlin in the 1020s:
Puddle Jump
Ink on paper, with
digital color overlay
12" x 9"

Foreword

> "Words have no power to impress the mind
> without the exquisite horror of their reality."
> – Edgar Allan Poe

As passionate editors and students of *New Plains Review,* The University of Central Oklahoma's literary journal, we have chosen the following written and visual work for their enticing originality, creativity, and urgency to be in print. We desire to engage our readers with thought-provoking emotion and discussion, while remaining true to the author's voice and intent, and to gather in unison a moving, memorable literary journal. This Fall, we have included a wide variety of material in our Poetry, Fiction, and Nonfiction sections. Inadvertently, we found ourselves being drawn to works that portray the darker side of the human mind and life. This may be evident considering our opening quote from Poe. While discussing these issues, we were convinced our readers would also be enraptured in the intensity of our writers' words. Our chosen authors and poets have written on diverse subjects such as suicide, depression, marriage, family dilemmas, death, society's obsession with beauty, murder and crime, imagination, and guilt. For our Special Section, Dr. Timothy Petete's students have submitted a variety of artistic representations discussing society's stereotypes, stereotypes in mental illnesses, feminism, and other imperative social issues. This issue's Visual Art section contains a wide variety of high contrast artwork and photography, portraits, and concept artwork. We have chosen to feature the talented Brian Forrest on our 1920s themed cover and divider artwork. On behalf of *New Plains Review,* we are pleased to present to you our Fall 2013 issue.

Christina Morel and Kaylee Kain,
Managing Editor and Poetry Editor

New Plains Review is published semiannually in the spring and fall by the University of Central Oklahoma and is staffed by faculty and students. We are committed to publishing high quality poetry, fiction, and creative non-fiction by established and emerging writers.

Contents

SPECIAL SECTION

NONFICTION

ABOUT THE CONTRIBUTORS

POETRY

Michael Hemmingson

The View, and then the Ashes

He looked so small in the viewing room,
embalmed, the bullet hole in his right temple "fixed,"
covered up with whatever make-up the experts use at the
funeral parlor. I was afraid to go near my father's body;
I do not know why. I could not look at him, stood
in a corner as my mother and brother approached
slowly like combatants holding up a white flag,
any anger and remorse set aside for this last moment
to speak to the body of the dead. He was no longer in great pain
and depression; his back had been straightened so
he could lay there, appearing at peace, not hunched over
like Jean Valjean carrying his burden in prison.
I said I forgave him for leaving the mess that all suicides are.
My mother cut off a snippet of his hair
and kissed his cold, pasty, white flesh, his
eyes closed—not as I saw him last, when the
Medical Examiners took him away, his eyes open,
staring up at nothing, that image I wish I had
not allowed myself to view. The next time I saw him,
he was inside a blue urn, ashes of what the broken body
once was, the incomplete scattered pieces of a life.

Lindsay Wilson

Elegy with no Shotgun

After everyone left me alone in her house,
I searched her closet first filled with sundresses
and the smell of old, floral perfume,

then mine, empty and dusty for years,
then the guest bedroom and the next,
through the hallway closets and into the garage

and its corners filled with boxes and tools,
but still no gun oil, no wooden handle,
and not even in the black widow shed

could I find my old 410 overlay,
but then finally beside the lawnmower
and its litter of dry, cut grass, I cleared away

that space in my mind and remembered
after her last failed suicide my father,
her long-ago ex, whose custody the state

had so embarrassingly placed her in,
had taken it and others to be destroyed.
The gravel floor crunched like gritting teeth

as I ran to her car and sped off into the Sierra
foothills for any road to announce itself,
to say left here, right there. What the fuck

did direction matter? So I wanted speed
under me, so I needed a dirt road, more gravel
and a sun to come down hard on every damn thing

at some dead end, some failed oil field lease,
some collapsed homestead, some place
to be in the world's teeth and chewed

until screaming took me, until only shooting
would do for the I-want-holes-in-everything mood
I was in. What do you give such hungry

and empty hands? So you've heard
this story. So your cynicism eats at you
like the bullet holes rusting through this fallen,

corrugated roof. Say so what. Say who cares.
Say death sleeps in everyone's bed.
What is it to you that once, as a boy,

I shot at clay pigeons and the ground
broke everyone? So she took me out from under
the gaze of the men who laughed

with each of my shots. Quail sprung from sage,
ran through the red rocks, and vanished
into the yellow bloom of rabbit brush.

She said, *easy, relax*. She said, *try again*.
But my anger swelled with everything I missed.
Once there was patience, a mother and son

alone, and the perfect complete arch of clay pigeons
that must break when finally their flight
takes them back to this hard, dry earth.

Christina Matekel-Gibson

Sitting in a Chair in a Therapist's Office

is just as relaxing and unnerving
as you would think.
"Why are you here?" she asks,
and "How do you feel?"

You avoid her gaze and think
instead about stampeding
through the room, ripping
shelves off the walls, watching
as books about accepting your childhood hit
the floor.

You want to appear as ravenous
as your soul tells you that you are.
You want to yank out your hair,
take your shoes off and throw
them in her face.

You want her to use her PhD to patch
up the gaping hole where she will cut
you open to replace
your anxieties with acceptance.

If you could, you would shout,
"I'M NOT OKAY!"
Because you aren't.
But instead you fold
your sweaty hands and say, "I don't know."

Jennifer L. Collins

Rooftop Observations

While I chat with strangers in the hotel over a breakfast of
   'cage-free eggs,'
A man jumps from the hotel's parking garage.

Buttering toast and pouring a second cup of coffee, I hear sirens,
   not knowing that nobody saw
his preparation or final arrival, just as, in our leisure, we ignore
   them, with a full day ahead.

Later, I tell another stranger, 'I'm glad I wasn't there to see
   him jump'
as we wonder together whether he managed to survive.

It's not unheard of we assure one another, with not a too-tall
   structure, after all, not really,
though we'll find out later he died, simply, alone and below us.

Today, I smiled and I laughed and I used the word 'survive' not in
   jest, an act I see now
as both rare and frightening and all too sure.

Now in this moment, with a glass of wine, I wonder not whether
   he survived, or could,
but whether he may, or whether others like him can.

I wonder whether a man who jumped today was a man I knew as
   a stranger yesterday,
or even still might know tomorrow in another form.

'Survival is not the question,' but gaining leverage over death,
   ignoring sirens in favor of
a stranger's smile, planning movement rather than stopping for
   breath, or despair.

Cindy King

To the Virgins

Painters wear white
   just to spite their paint—

Some wear it to weddings, even when
   they are not the bride.

Most have turned down more beds
   than a hotel housekeeper, take

their one-night stands
   lying down—

Many place faith in champagne
   pledges: the bottle's broken

promise to become beach glass—
   But few have learned that divorce

can undo a marriage no more
   than a freezer can unbake a cake.

Sarah Katharina Kayß

I'm Sick

I have *post academic stress disorder*
and no one can help me
haven't had a proper job in years, haven't had any money (either)
in return lots of ideas (which won't pay the bills)

my relatives think: I'm doing something illegal
I think: I wish I had been born two hundred years ago
everyone thinks: something's wrong
stare into n-o-t-h-i-n-g: it's thousand o'clock. again

working effectively…sleeping
all the time. a complete waste of time…makes me aggressive
even worse: eating, showering and so on
talking to people, who think *Habermas* is a funny dialect

everything is like counting calories: it's always at the back of your mind
liquid aggregate through the veins: ecstasy (or similar)
(on a completely natural path)…a source of income, sort of
strategic thinking. always & everywhere (even at funerals)

healing is not on the cards
at some point I will be cremated. just like that.
without analysis. no diagnostics. snuffed out. poor fool.

Brianna Pike

Starling

For Roger and Beth Young

This morning I shot a starling straight from the sky.
The shiny, black bastard drove the sparrows and wrens
from your carefully kept feeders, then strutted
about the branches of our old apple tree.

You do not approve, Beth. Your gentle soul gives grace
to all creatures, even your sisters who just arrived.
You are pouring tea as I walk around the front of our house,
shotgun resting over my right shoulder.

Three sisters swoop down on your small
frame, pulling at your arms, pressing against your back.
Their cackling disrupts our quiet home, dark
eyes move over our stone floors,

pine paneled walls, and the small, cast iron stove
smoking away in the corner. You look away,
your eyes light, but your mouth a thin, rigid
line slicing your face in two.

As the youngest you bear their burden, the blame
for lost children and broken husbands. With each passing
summer they move farther from you,
carrying their judgment in packed bags,

buried beneath silk stockings and picture frames.
Their misery will grow like your carefully tended
lilies, and you, my love, will suffer.
But for now, you will serve sweet tea and yellow

cake. You will forgive, slip me a quick smile as
all four of you come round back, talking peonies,
and oriental poppies, just in time to watch me
string the starling up high, a warning

to his flock. As I descend from our tree,
three sets of eyes meet mine, uncertain
in the harsh summer sun. They move to bird's
broken black body, swaying.
My warning is also clear.

Ryan Havely

The Woman With No Eyes

pointed her Nissan at the concrete leg
of a severed train bridge on Jefferson
last Thursday between 11:30
and midnight. I wasn't slouched
in a dark booth in Carmine's struggling
with a last carafe of sangria, waiting
for a taxi when she walked into the warm
night between 11:00 and 11:30,
but somebody was. Somebody saw her
fumble in the summer-black parking lot
for her keys. I wasn't there but maybe you were.
Maybe you heard her fighting on the phone,
her husband's static anger muffled
with humidity, or maybe she was laughing
and you thought, *how nice*. Maybe she blinked
a dream too long, or tried missing
the halogen eyes of a fragile animal. Perhaps
stuck in the mouth of a too-hot summer
we all feel a bit like dying. You want to

know her as a daughter or sister
and I can tell you things that would make you sad.
You want to know if her blistered fingers
still squeezed the wheel as those men hoisted
a braided mess of Japanese steel
up the bank, or when, after drowning,
sunny hair will rust and ride the undercurrent
in clumps to Tennessee? You want to know
what terrible minnows would take only eyes
or if her gray lips pursed in fear
when the towline broke and she rolled back
to death again. I will not say what I know.
I'll tell you I learned to fish
for rainbows in the fast water,
that she was not a mother
and there was no car seat in the back,
if there had been I'd tell you it was empty.
I'll tell you I woke with a headache,
and walked the riverbank this morning
because summer was so hot
I knew something had to be wrong.

Ralph Monday

Song in Burnt Umber

Winter is coming.
The energy leaves the
mantis,
The girl leaves
high school,
Throws away her books.

The mother cooks no more
Meals.
The boy abandons
Church,
Finds energy in
Wine.

Thinking of different days,
The husband spies the wife
One burnt night,
Loves her no more.
The mistress is a serpent
Temptress.

The minister,
Clothed in umber,
Cannot tongue sin.
Shoes paw at the ice,
Patterns fading into the
Trees.

Mantis, girl, mother, boy
Husband, mistress, minister,
No one knows from where
Their tongued hieroglyphs
Deciphered
The center.

Anthony Rintala

The Saturday

I can point at the body's twist, crimped by the wheel,
white socks swelling where blood ruffles blackberry
on her dark leg; she writhes. Not blood on the bone, but cherry
syrup drizzled, waffle wet over the ooze of her: here is horror.

Point at the Sedan, rocking on the squall of its brakes
hurked to a stop as if it had at all sped and not rolled slow
over the tight pigtails which unfolded from the back door
while it K-turned—the bump of her, the squeal, the rock.

Or at the Cadillac on the highway, uninvolved, unseen
but by me, it's own thing, which at that moment, purring past,
threw its hood, a screaming gator jaw smile, which, one-
two, smashed the glass and flipped over, a curling leaf.

I can't point at the clench, the resistant second, or dad, tugging
me with the backseat blanket to swaddle the spilling girl, to
drape her—his heroic suddenness, my shocking clutch. *I'm cold!*
Harrowed by the horror of it, so I focus on the girl, the road.

Daniel Romo

Guided by Dragons Instead of Hybrids

for Hannah

I float over the city while holding a bouquet of balloons. Hands grasping ribbon and fragments of sky. A bird's-eye view of domesticity. Rooftops lose their shape and resemble outstretched angles. Busy streets become nothing more than intersecting lines. I soar over neighbors' backyards and applaud the consistency of their landscape. Uniformed shrubbery improving property values. Yet I pity the residents. Self-contained in crown molding-nine-to-five lives, never to taste the origin of clouds. Feet planted in suburbs they're destined to die in. It starts to rain, but not even the threat of lightning striking me down can ground me. I face droplets, head-on, knowing that is not enough water to drown in.

Brad Garber

We Only Hire Beautiful People

Only those with advanced degrees
   who have certain sensibilities.

This is not a garage or a place where
   people spit or discuss irrelevant topics
where symmetry is lost or odors disgust.

This is a palace of aesthetic perfection
   a cathedral of white marbled halls
where small feet walk from room
   to silent room and broad shoulders
bare in filtered light become posters
   to adorn the buses that carry ordinary
grunts through their pathetic and repulsive
   sad shadowy terrible lives.

Please smile at me again arch
   your back and neck and flex
those oiled muscles in your awesome arms
   rise up on your perfect toes
look into the fan.

How you look will serve you well
   like this rose I hand you
when you sign the contract.

Place it in water and look at it
   Until the petals fall off.

Meeah Williams

Bus of the Dead

There was a dead guy
sitting on the bus
in front of me tonight.
He was calling the office
on his cell phone
giving some last minute
instructions to some poor
bastard who worked for him.
He was talking in such a loud,
obnoxious voice I turned
to look if he was disturbing
anyone else besides me. But the woman
across the aisle reading
the *NY Times* was dead
too and so were the couple
chatting behind her. In fact,
it seemed as if I were the only
living person on the whole
fucking bus. Naturally,
I began to get worried.
I was speeding down the
turnpike in a busload of dead
folks past a landscape
of petrochemical drums and

mobster swampland. And
then I made the mistake
of looking in the rear view
mirror and seeing the bus
driver's eyes looking directly
at me. I knew right then I
wasn't going home alive
that night. It didn't make a
difference whether he drove
off the bridge or slammed into
a cement mixer. I looked at
my pale reflection in the
darkening window and saw
what he saw: another pale-
faced dead commuter on
his way home to his house,
his family, his dinner, his TV,
and his moonlit sexless bed.
I wanted to laugh, but the dead
don't laugh they just sort of
unhinge their jaws in mute surprise.
Besides, even among the dead
I prefer not to seem insane.

John McKernan

What Happened to all the Murderers and Thieves Who Spoke Latin?

You call this a dead language?
Looks real enough to me

This semi-infinite encyclopedia
Of lies & murders
Betrayals & tortures

It's easy to imagine
Caesar stuttering
When that knife sliced his way
And the rust just kept on rusting

I actually stole
A large pebble from Rome
A cobblestone
Could have got twenty years in prison   I'm told
Had it ground into a fine sand for an hourglass

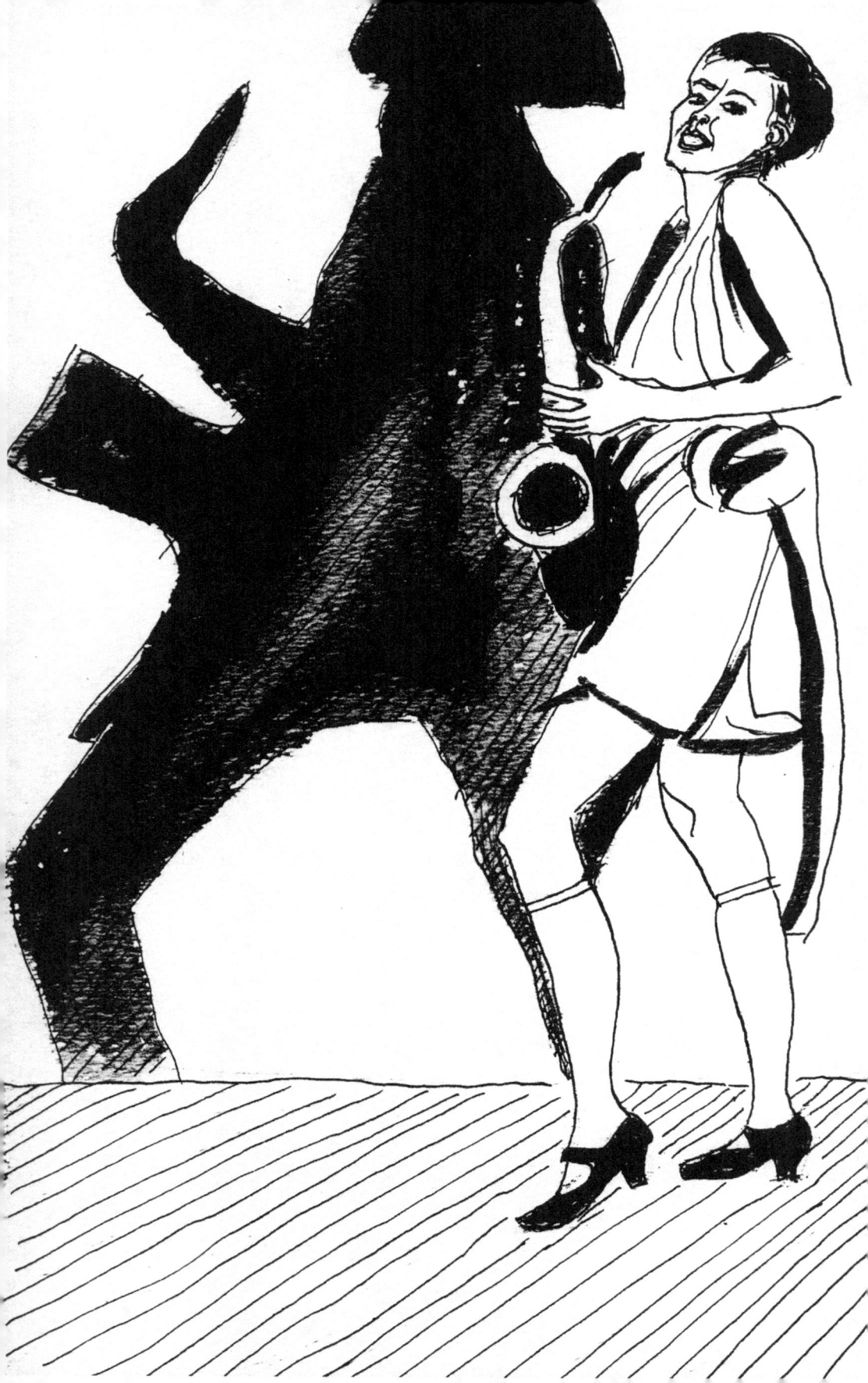

FICTION

Brian Forrest
Berlin in the 1020s: Show Girls 2
Ink on paper
12" x 9"

Wendy C. Williford

The One About The Pig and The Silk Purse

A wedding or a murder would take place today. Either way, at least the clergy would be there.

Iris made her way across the yard with fire in her eyes. It was high time everyone took the events of this day seriously. It wasn't every day she got married and if those stupid idiots she called brothers did anything to mess this up, there would be hell to pay.

Iris threw open the barn door. As she made her way across the room, she gripped the handle of her bucket of water. She squinted, searched the musty room with the little light that the cracks of the weathered wood provided. In the far corner of the barn, she found her target. Smiling, she approached the mound that moaned and undulated beneath an old, dirty blanket. Without warning, she heaved back the bucket and let them have it. The water hit and the moans turned to shrieks of surprise and confusion. The blanket flew back to reveal the biggest bane of her existence: her oldest brother Seamus.

"Iris! What the feck are you doing?" he yelled, staring at her through the long dark bangs which dripped over his eyes. He pushed his hair back and squinted at his sister, relieved it was only her.

"Seamus McMurrough, unless you want another bucket of water, you better start remembering what today is!" Iris peered down at him with a ferocity in her green eyes she had rarely shown to another living soul. Only five and a half feet of her towered over him and her long dirty-blonde hair was tied up in haphazardly placed curlers. She couldn't hurt a fly soaking wet, but it never once stopped her from thinking she could thrash him anytime she pleased. Just as she was about to throw the bucket at him, a blonde headed girl emerged from the blanket and gave Iris a friendly smile.

"And Molly Byrne," Iris said with a nod. A hint of superiority rang in her voice. "Can't say I'm surprised to see you here. Although, I thought it was Dougal you were under these days."

Molly took no notice of the insult. Instead, she adjusted the wet blanket around her chest and moved the hair from her sweaty face. "No, Dougal and I stopped weeks ago. Hey, Iris, I hear you're getting married. Congratulations."

"Thanks, Molly, that's my plan if my eejit brothers stop feckin' around!" Iris shot a dirty look in Seamus' direction.

"Alright, alright," Seamus said. He looked around the barn floor, trying to remember where his pants had fallen.

"Hey, Iris," Molly said, taking Iris' attention once again. "I hear you're having a baby."

Iris's eyes widened and her face flushed. "You told her!" She reared back and flung the bucket at Seamus, which struck him in the middle of the forehead. Before he hit the ground, it actually surprised him—the precision of her aim. He could hear Molly's laughter and Iris' annoyed cries. By the time his vision returned to normal, Iris had left the barn.

Iris made her way across the back yard and cursed the day Seamus was born. She wondered what ungodly sin she committed to be plagued with one of the stupidest brothers in all of Ireland, much less County Clare. She couldn't fathom it. Of all things, she was a good Catholic girl. She attended mass, at least the important ones. She minded her mother, when it was convenient and never neglected her studies. It wasn't until the morning sickness started six weeks ago when she realized she might have strayed off the righteous path. It had to be a curse, she concluded. It happened to all good Irish families. Just look at the Kennedys of America. Only the McMurroughs were not cursed with untimely deaths, just stupid men.

Iris headed to the little house she had lived in all of her life. The quaint homestead wasn't the fanciest, with the daisies and wildflowers that sporadically grew in the garden, or the lopsided gate that opened to the broken cobblestone walkway. The hedgerow wasn't always neatly trimmed and the branches of the downy birch and holly trees hung too low. No, it might not be the grandest, but the house and the land belonged to her family, which made them feel like one of the richest in the county.

Before Iris reached the house, she caught sight of her second brother, Dougal, strolling through the yard. Dougal was the second oldest and just as wanting for intellect as the others. He was a big brute and lazy to boot, so it didn't surprise Iris that he wasn't setting up the tables near the garden like she ordered him to do two hours ago. He was accompanied by Tommy O'Dwyer, a boy she knew from school and one of the first boys she had ever kissed. Although the kiss was simply a dare from a friend, it left a lasting impression on Tommy. His presence struck her a bit odd, but the preparations of the wedding weighed on her mind, so she barely gave it a second thought.

"Iris," Dougal called to her. Iris stopped in her tracks. She turned, let out a deep sigh, and gave him a scornful look. Dougal was not the least bit aware of how irritated his sister's mood had turned over the last hour. "Look who came to pay you a visit."

Iris stared at Tommy with the same indifference as she had always shown him. Tommy gazed back with a nervous smile. It didn't escape her notice, the sweat beaded across his forehead or the wilted flowers he gripped between his dirty fingers.

"Iris, you sure are looking grand these days," Tommy said. His feeble attempt to give her a winning smile failed miserably. She could barely see past his crooked teeth, freckly complexion and dark stringy hair.

"What is it you want, Tommy?" Iris' growing hostility threw Tommy slightly off. He looked to Dougal for moral support, but all Dougal did was give him a shove on the shoulder. Tommy took in a deep breath, straightened himself up and stepped toward Iris with as much courage as he could muster.

"Iris McMurrough, I've come here to ask you to be my wife!"

Her astonishment was the only thing that saved her from laughing in Tommy's face. "Why would I want to be marrying you, Tommy O'Dwyer?"

Tommy was at a loss for words. He hadn't expected Iris to question his motives. When Dougal talked him into this venture at the pub the night before, he considered it a done deal. He timidly looked to Dougal for help with the answer.

"Did he set you up to this?" she asked Tommy. She turned to Dougal, whose confident demeanor hid the fact it had been ages since he had had a bright idea. "Dougal, how many times do I have to tell you that I'm marrying William!"

"But are you sure you ought to be doing that? I don't think God would be very pleased if you did." Dougal leaned in closer to Iris and lowered his voice to save Tommy from the awful truth of the situation. "William is a fine lad, but he's Protestant. And more than that, Tommy is Irish."

"William is Irish, too!" Her fists balled up, her fingernails dug into her palm. Dougal was just as big and as heavily built as Seamus, but she knew she'd have him flat on his back with one swing alone.

"Yeah, but you said he was born in Monaghan. That's far too close to the border for my liking."

"I was born in Kilkenny," Tommy proudly announced.

Iris' aggravation approached a boiling point. Her eye twitched. Is this what a nervous breakdown feels like? And the true horror of reality hit her. It was nothing more than a flash in the corner of her eye, but it was enough. A whole new panic set in. Eoin, the youngest of the brothers and undoubtedly the most handsome, came walking across the yard in their direction, naked as the day he was born and just as proud as he pleased.

"Where are your clothes?" Iris quickly took off her apron and tossed it at him. She wasn't sure where it hit him. In fact, she didn't want to know.

Eoin greeted Tommy and Dougal and made the best use of the apron. "Ma told me take a bath, and so, I did."

"Are you that stupid, or do you have to be reminded to put some feckin' clothes on afterward?" Iris could envision how the day would play out. She would have the wedding from Hell, William's family would realize how redneck she and her family were and she would have to live the rest of her life feeling inferior to them. Worse than that, her children would have to suffer the consequence as well.

Iris felt a strange whirlwind surround her. Hopelessness set in. By this time, Seamus had emerged from the barn. At least he was clothed, she thought. He laughed when he saw Eoin. He needed no explanation when he saw Tommy O'Dwyer standing beside Dougal with the flowers in his hand. Iris' irritation thrilled him more than anything. He couldn't pay for better entertainment.

"I'm going to murder you all," she said. Her voice had a strange calmness to it, the kind of tranquility which mad minds often have before the eruption.

"Iris, be a good girl," Seamus said with a wink, "Or I might just have to have a chat with Father Flannery, let him know you're up the duff and that's why you insisted on getting married so sudden."

The very thought had just the reaction he hoped for when a familiar fire flashed through Iris' eyes. Yet, as it burned out, she took a deep breath and calmed herself. When she gave him a sinister grin, her eyes reminded him that she was, in fact, a McMurrough after all and could be just as mischievous as he.

"Hey, Dougal, guess who I found in the barn this morning, grunting it up with Molly Byrne?"

Dougal, amidst another scheme to get Tommy to propose to Iris, looked up when he heard Molly's name. The way Iris smirked and the guilty way Seamus shook his head was the only explanation he needed.

"You bastard!" Dougal rushed him before Seamus could make an attempt to block. They were on the ground, wrestling, throwing punches and yelling out obscenities in a split second. They argued over the social status of Molly Byrne, as if either of them had the right to claim her. Just as Dougal got Seamus in a mastered sleeper lock, the entire fracas was interrupted by the howling scream of their mother. Iris turned in shock, but relieved her one true ally had finally arrived. Dougal eased his grip around Seamus' neck as the blood drained from his face. Eoin made an honest attempt to cover himself with the apron and Tommy O'Dwyer simply stood there, smiling like the biggest eejit in the county. He actually bothered to straighten his dirty tie.

Maddie McMurrough was not a woman to be trifled with. The stern look she gave them put the fear of the Lord into them all. Her face, much older than her actual years and the severity of her stance was enough to tell anyone she was truly the head of this family. She was like a tower among them and her rigid posture was just as looming.

"What is going on here?" The question was not meant to be answered. Her powerful eyes met them one by one, sending them into an uncomfortable state of calm. This was a woman who knew the meaning of strife, although she rarely spoke of it.

Maddie shook her head in shame, unable to hide her disappointment. "I thank the Lord that your da is six feet under and not here to see the bunch of eejits his namesakes have become." She made the sign of the cross and bowed her head for a moment. Everyone did the same, more out of obedience to their mother rather than quiet reflection on their father.

"Are you all done with your messing about?" The severity of her countenance never once relented. None of her children looked at her. They all stared at the ground, shifting from side to side, and eyes dashing to one another. She waited for each of them to nod or give some indication they understood.

"Now, we have a wedding to prepare for. Dougal, get the tables like you were told. Seamus, finish setting the chairs and then go pick up Father Flannery. If you mention a word to the Father about your sister's condition, you have me to answer to." Her eyes met up with Eoin. She shook her head and rolled her eyes. "Eoin, for God's sake, put some clothes on. You're not half the man your father was, so there's no use in displaying your arse to everyone in the county."

The brothers dispersed and swaggered past Iris with good-hearted smiles on their faces. The anger still burned in her eyes although she was on the verge of tears.

"Iris, go take your grandfather his tea. I'll see to it you get married today."

Iris nodded and left her mother. The day would be ruined, she knew it. Why, for once, couldn't her brothers just act normal? It wasn't much to ask. Every attempt she had ever made to better herself, they were there, dragging her back down, never letting her forget she was just a country girl from County Clare.

She could just imagine the stories that would come of it. She had put so much care into planning this wedding—but it would end with a murder now. It was inevitable. The most special day of days was well on the way of being nothing more than a sad anecdote to be mulled over down at the pub. She could hear the voices, the men chatting and pondering over the day young Iris McMurrough went mad:

"Did you hear the one about the girl in County Clare?" Paddy O'Brien would say as he sipped his ale.

"She went mad one day and murdered her brothers," Sean McGoorty would add as he puffed his pipe.

"A bunch of stupid gits, the whole lot of them," Eamon McGlynn would throw in and all would nod and take another sip of their drinks. No doubt someone would eventually write a drinking song in her honor the night before her execution. It would be sung throughout the county and most certainly spread as far as County Cork, if the tune was pleasant enough.

Iris made the decision right then not to be remembered in this way. She took a calming breath and entered the house. At least there was one person who could give her a moment of serenity in this totally mad day.

Iris handed her grandfather his cup of tea and adjusted the blanket around his legs.

"Can you see alright?" she asked him as she pulled the curtain away from the window. He had a beautiful view into the backyard. Iris hated he would miss her wedding, but his old and worn out body wasn't strong enough to handle all of the excitement. The one consolation she had was he'd be able to watch from his room upstairs.

"Are you having a party?"

Iris gave him a gentle smile. She had to explain this to him nearly every day. "Gran, I'm getting married today."

"Are you now? Isn't that grand."

Iris pulled up a chair beside him and held his hand.

"Who are you marrying?"

"A very handsome man by the name of William Griffin."

"William?" His eyebrow raised and he leaned forward a bit. "Is he Protestant?"

"Of course not." Iris was lying, but she didn't really feel guilty. William was on the way to converting to Catholicism, so she didn't see any harm in it. "In fact, he's related to Michael Collins himself."

Gran's eyes lit up. "Is he now?"

"Aye, his great-grandfather was Collins' second cousin."

"You don't say."

Iris was happy to see her grandfather smile so brightly. Heritage and lineage were extremely important to him. If she didn't know better, knowing he would have a great-grandchild related to Collins himself would allow him to die a happy man. Of course, it was another lie. She would have felt guilty if she didn't know he would forget every bit of the conversation in a few hours.

"Will he treat you good?"

"Of course he will." Iris stirred his tea and helped him take a sip.

"And will he stay away from the drink?"

"He's promised, not a drop."

"Grand."

Iris adjusted a shawl across his shoulders and looked out the window. Progress was finally being made. Dougal had nearly all of the tables ready. Eoin was dressed and arranging the folding chairs in front of the garden. Even Tommy O'Dwyer made himself busy, spreading out the tablecloths and fixing the flower center pieces. It made her smile. Even though she had never looked at Tommy romantically, he was a good lad, after all, incapable of holding a grudge.

The aroma coming from the kitchen below filled the room. The smell of the ham and beef roasting in the oven hung in the air. The smell of Irish stew and gooseberry crumble made her feel warm and peaceful inside. It wasn't until this moment she realized she was leaving all of this. Today, she was getting married and leaving the warmth and security of her home behind. In a matter of hours she would be married. In a matter of months, she would be a mother. Everything had happened so fast, she had barely had time to adjust to a new life and role.

Iris let out a deep sigh and squeezed her grandfather's hand. He rocked back and forth in his chair, staring out the window still trying to make sense of what was going on outside.

"Iris, will you still come and visit me when you are off and married?"

She wiped a tear from the corner of her eye and braved a smile. "Every Sunday, after church."

Gran sensed the nervousness which had come over her. "Iris, will you sing with me before you go and get married?"

Iris nodded. She went down to her knees and placed her arms in his lap and laid her head down, a tradition they shared together for as long as she could remember.

"A Nation once again......"

The wedding went off without a hitch, much to Iris' surprise. For the first time in her life, the brothers McMurrough acted like perfect gentlemen. When Father Flannery asked if there were any objections, there wasn't a single peep out of any of them. Iris was on edge the entire ceremony, waiting for one of them to shout about something or threaten to punch someone, but they didn't. She was grateful and would give extra thanks next Sunday at church, for God had finally given them all a bit of sense.

After the cake and champagne had been served, Iris danced with her husband. It greatly calmed her, seeing he was actually comfortable in her environment. His parents, she noticed, were not so much, but they were making the attempt by chatting gaily with her mother and Father Flannery. Iris let go a deep, relaxing sigh of relief. She laid her head on William's shoulder. Finally, normality had come. Her brothers hadn't embarrassed her, she hadn't murdered them and she wasn't going to jail.

"Excuse us, brother."

Seamus' voice addressed William. Iris came out of her temporary stupor. She opened her eyes, lifted her head to see her brothers standing shoulder to shoulder, staring at William. The serious tones of their expressions sent her into panic. Impending doom came over her again. This was it—this was going to be the moment they embarrassed her. At least William was legally bound to her now.

"What's wrong?" She barely got the words out. Her lips actually quivered.

"First order of business," Seamus said. He took an intimidating stance against William. "You marrying our sister means you're Irish now." Confusion swept over William's face. Iris squeezed his hand as he opened his mouth to question him. "So from this day on, we're calling you Liam."

"Aye, Liam." It was Eoin who chimed in. He rarely had an original thought; he just mimicked whatever the others said.

"And secondly," Seamus continued, "It wouldn't be right if we sent you off without an appropriate wedding present."

They all grinned like idiots. Iris' hands were sweating. Her heart jumped in her chest as they broke their formation and from behind them a pig came forth. The huge sow nearly stood up to Iris's waist. The pig was immaculately clean, in fact still wet from its bath. If Iris didn't know any better, she could have sworn the pig smelled of gallunac. And around its huge neck was a large, red silk ribbon with a red silk leash.

"If you're going to be a farmer's wife," Dougal said with a smirk, "it's only befitting that we start you off with your first animal."

Iris felt the madness set in again. Her only regret was that she didn't live closer to Dublin. Everyone knew the better prison was in Dublin. And they probably wouldn't execute a pregnant girl.

"Dougal, you bleedin' eejit," she said under her breath. She tried her best to maintain her composure in front of her husband. "You know we'll be living in a flat in town. *William* works in his father's hotel."

"So, does that mean you don't want the pig?" Eoin asked, smirking that same idiot grin of his.

"What am I gonna do with a pig?"

Dougal shrugged. "Lots of things. Either hunt for truffles or make a Sunday ham when we come and visit you."

"Before you start getting all high and mighty, why don't you take a closer look at this pig," Seamus spouted out. This time, his voice was as stern as it had ever been. Just the change in his demeanor made Iris a little more curious. Iris unclenched her fist and looked down at the pig. It was at this point she noticed a matching red purse hanging from the sash around its neck.

"What's that?" Her eyes turned upward to Seamus and Dougal. Curiosity was replaced with skepticism.

Dougal and Seamus shrugged. "Don't know," Seamus said. "I think it came with the pig."

Iris leaned down and untied the ribbon and the purse from the pig's neck. She immediately noted how bulky, yet light the purse was. She struggled for a moment with the carefully tied knot. What she found inside astounded her.

It was money. A large wad of money.

"What is this?" Iris' voice quivered again.

Eoin shrugged, "Don't know. It must have come with the pig."

Iris and William counted the money as fast as their shaky fingers would allow. Then they counted it again just to make sure. Each time, they came up with a total of £400.

"I don't understand," she said. Her eyes were wide and her heart fluttered inside her chest. She gripped William's hand to the point of nearly breaking it. Her eyes welled up with tears.

"You're our baby sister, Iris," Seamus explained, his voice slightly softer than it had been before.

Iris was more worried for their souls now.

"Did you rob the pub?" She could barely speak for the lump in her throat.

"We've been saving it for a long time," Dougal explained. "We knew this day would come and you'd need it. Liam's our brother now, too. And when Dubhlainn gets here, this will help him as well."

Iris managed a laugh when she saw William struggle to make sense of it all. "Who's Dubhlainn?"

"That's what they think to name our baby," Iris smiled and kissed her husband.

"You eejit," Eoin turned to Seamus and hit him on the arm. "You said we could name it Fergus."

Iris laughed and squeezed her husband's hand and led him away. She was afraid William might somehow get mixed in when the first punch flew. She didn't want to spend her honeymoon nursing a black eye and bloody lip. From the look of bewilderment that covered his face, it pleased her to know she would spend every day explaining the brothers McMurrough to her husband and children. It was going to be a daunting task, but it was one she would do with joy.

"Did you hear the one about the pig and the silk purse?" Paddy O'Brien said, as he handed Declan McKenna another pint.

"Aye," Eamon McGlynn said with a smile as he lit his pipe. The pub filled with the sweet smell of tobacco. *"It's a grand story. Let's hear it again."*

Nick Bertelson

Missteps

Jordan Profaci was reliable, always ready to work, always there. Too bad he was useless as tits on a boar. Growing up, the kids called him "Schnitzel Fingers" because Jordan's fingers looked like tiny links of cured meat with the dexterity to match. The Schnitzel Fingers of 1943 was the kid our teacher paraded around at least once a month to show what happened to students who stashed cold-meat sandwiches in their desks. I always heard him crinkling the oil paper while Miss Blovey went on about Eastern Europe cities: these statue-filled destinations that would soon be reduced to rubble by American bombs.

"Jordan!" I whispered. I was never one to call my friend Schnitzel Fingers. "Jordan! She's gonna catch you."

"Not if you'd quit your smartass whispering..." he said.

Then every single tiny spine in that room straightened as Miss Blovey struck the side of her desk with her yardstick, her eyes two coals burning hot for pudgy Jordan Profaci.

After school, I told my mom about Jordan. She said, "You want to know why you're a good kid, Tory? Because you always help the underdog."

"But he got the switch anyway," I said.

"You tried," she said. "That's all that matters."

We lived near Prospect Park, Mother and I, and she often took me there to do my schoolwork while she read her magazines. World War II had silenced the city, especially in the evenings when wives hunkered down near their radio. Meanwhile, the birds above us twitted away irreverently. We always sat in the grass near a monument commemorating the fall of a tree by American troops to obstruct British forces during the Revolutionary War. In light of the war occurring overseas then, it made the bloodshed that first freed our country seem naive and cartoonish. Cutting down a tree to stop the bad guy—like something Bugs Bunny might do to stop Elmer Fudd.

I'd read in some colossal book that in World War I the Germans filled the air with a gas that made the American troops flop on the ground like fish out of water. At dinner, I asked my mother if the Germans still gassed the Americans.

"What book said that?" she asked.

"One at school, in the library. They won't let you check it out. Only look at it."

"They shouldn't even let you do that," she said.

I took a bite of ham loaf, trying to figure out how to rid my plate of its cabbage without her seeing. The bowl of beets was something I'd have to reckon with, storing each bite in my cheek and breathing slowly until the urge to vomit had subsided and I could swallow however many bites she'd forced me to take. Mom had a garden just off our complex's thoroughfare. Beets, she insisted, would make me a man. "Like your father."

She took a letter out from her apron: "Maybe I shouldn't read this," she said. "Not with those ideas floating around in your head."

"No! Read it now!" I said. "World War One? What's that?"

The envelope had already been opened. There were always two letters from Dad, one meant just for Mom, with all the gushy stuff, and one meant for me. She unfolded the letter methodically.

"Dear Torrence," she read. I hated the sound of my full name. *"It's surprisingly chilly in Antibes this time of year."*

"Where's Antibes?" I asked.

"If we're gonna play that game again, I'm not reading it."

I packed my mouth full of ham loaf and stared at the beet in its bowl, like a filleted heart.

"The resort we've been furloughed in has a pool overlooking the Mediterranean. In the morning, steam rises off it and you can see more guys coming in by ship..."

Jordan's hands changed, they got bigger, morphing into knobby-knuckled, thick-nailed monstrosities, but of course his nickname stuck. The Schnitzel Fingers of 1955 looked like an overweight parody of tough-guy Italians. He always had a soft pack of cigarettes rolled into his sleeve and a head of jet black hair so greased back it looked like the toe of a well-polished boot. But he was thick, thick in the body, thick in the head. His shirts were always coming untucked, exposing his stretch-marked belly, and the boots he insisted on wearing slipped on the slightest incline.

We were smoking cigarettes in his uncle's dark car.

"Schnitzel Fingers won't cut it," I said. "It's cumbersome. And awfully close to snitch: Schnitzel, snitch. I don't know."

He watched through the windshield, half-listening to me. We were waiting for the front door of Morran's row-house to open.

42

"Just drive the car," he said.

That was all I ever had to do: just drive the car, just watch the door, just hold the flashlight. "Just" implied that I had one responsibility, one task, but that's all it amounted to: an implication. Soon enough, I'd be doing seventy down Queens or barricading the door with a mattress or turning the flashlight around and cracking someone's nose with it.

Jordan snapped off a mouthful of apple:

"You're the only person I know who thinks about shit like that," he said. "Peoples' names and shit. What's it to you?"

"What if I just called you Fingers?" I snapped my fingers.

"What if people called you 'Shut-Your-Yapper'?"

"See, it's the brevity thing you need to work on."

"There he is!" Jordan whispered. "Morran."

He lowered himself in his seat, staring over the dashboard. I ducked and looked through the steering wheel. The man emerged from the door, flipping off the light behind him and plopping on a fedora. Jordan's eyes lit up with anxiety, a primal look of panic. I did not like that look. Not because it made Jordan intimidating, but because it made him look like prey being chased. It meant things would not go as planned. The man started his car and pulled out into the street.

"Go, go," Jordan said. "Go!"

I snuffed my cigarette out in the ashtray, exhaling and putting the car in drive.

"How about Wiener Fingers," I said.

"Just drive the car!"

Unlike my own father, Jordan's dad had not joined the war effort on account of his bad arm: this hapless thing that dangled from his side and made for another Profaci appendage reminiscent of odd, yet edible meat. He worked as a fishmonger on the upper east side, and, as a kid, I found it odd that Jordan's father made a living as a fishwife while my mother came home from the smelting factory night after night with burn marks on her arms; the liquid scrap metal always sloshed out of the furnace, scabbing constellations into her skin.

But Jordan's father at least made a legitimate living, which was more than Jordan's grandfather could say. The elder Profaci was not spoken of in Jordan's home. He was, as Jordan's father put it, "a crook." Still, the old man's presence resonated throughout their family whether they wanted it to or not, especially when Jordan's grand-father did something extraordinary, like send tickets to a Broadway performance, not just reserving enough seats for his kids and grand-kids, but getting a whole row or two near the stage. He once bought so many tickets, in fact, that Jordan invited me along one night near the end of the school year, and my mother, eager for me to experience a bit of culture (especially *free* culture), allowed me to go.

Jordan's mother accompanied us, along with his sisters. In Time Square there stood a huge sign of FDR. Above him, it read, "The USO deserves the support of every American citizen." I looked at Jordan's mother, expecting her to see the sign and hang her head given that her family (in comparison to mine) did very little in sup-port of the war effort. Of course, it was a childish notion of what should happen. When she finally did look at the sign, she showed no remorse and I wondered if she considered her husband's job hawking wide-eyed fish to be something of a patriotic duty.

The musical was called *Those Endearing Young Charms,* a title made ironic by the main character, this guy named Hank, a no-strings-attached kind of guy. His friend, this milquetoast Army private, introduces Hank to his girlfriend back in The States while the men furloughed. Helen was the girl's name, and she had lips redder than any beet in Mom's garden. Not long after the play starts, Hank ends up stealing off with her. I was pretty caught up in Helen for a time too, until my attention shifted to Jordan's grandfather: a stony man with no neck and this cigar that lit up his whole face when he puffed on it. He trumped the show in my opinion, simply in the way he whispered to the men around him, how they smiled and nodded, pointing at the stage, their knuckles and necks heavy with bibelots of gold and silver. I was so caught up in him that, by the time the musical ended, I didn't know whether Helen went back to her upstanding beau or stuck with bawdy old Hank.

That night, we rode in one of the elder Profaci's cars instead of taking the train home. The driver took me right to my house, even opened the car door for me. When I went to say goodbye to Jordan, he was asleep on his mother's lap, those fat fingers gnarling the fabric of her dress. The driver escorted me up the stoop and rang the bell. My mother was at the door in seconds, clutching me, crying.

"It's okay, Ma," I said, nearly laughing at her overreaction. "I'm back home. Nothing happened."

But then I saw the flag on the table, folded in a triangle. I'd read about those in that big library book too.

Jordan cowered inside the car. I stared at the motionless, hog-tied lump in the trunk, a bloody fedora sitting neatly atop it. Back in the driver's seat, I removed my gloves and replaced each of my rings on their respective fingers. Meanwhile, Jordan snatched the cigarettes off the dash, but his hands were shaking so bad that I had to light his for him. I took one too, and we both sat in the car for a moment. Occasionally, I went to speak, but stopped myself and took a drag instead. I suppose I was thankful Jordan wasn't crying this time. It was a step in the right direction.

Finally, Jordan said something: "Well, I can't go to my cousin's place like this."

"I don't know where you want me to go," I said. "We ain't going all the way to your place for a pair of pants. If we were going to your place, we'd just wait for the call there."

"I don't know. A store."

"There's nothing open this time a night," I said.

"Let's get the pair out of the trunk."

"What pair in the trunk?"

"He was about my size," Jordan said.

"Jesus, so when I put a gun to his head, you piss yourself. But now you got no problem stealing Morran's pants."

"I can't go to my cousin's covered in piss. It'll take two minutes."

I pulled the car into the parking lot of a dry-cleaning joint, wheeling around to the back where a row of windows revealed just how much intricate equipment was required to clean a pair of trousers.

"If only they were open," Jordan said, staring inside longingly.

"Two minutes," I said.

He got out. I turned on the radio. When the tubes warmed up, I heard a Mills Brothers song from my childhood: *"If I broke your heart last night it's because I love you most of all."*

I watched Jordan manhandle Morran. He untied his hands and shook him free from the sack. The car rocked like someone putting the moves on his sweetheart. Once in awhile, I looked around to make sure no one's car pulled in the lot.

"Tory!" Jordan whispered. "Tory! A little help."

Jordan had the right idea to begin with: just wrest the guy out the back of the trunk and slip his pants off. But for some reason he'd started walking around with Morran upright until he had him down to his boxer-shorts and sock-clips. I lit a cigarette, unsure when to start giving a fuck about this situation. Then they both flopped to the ground, one then the other, Jordan then Morran. It knocked the wind out of Jordan, who laid on the ground, moaning. A dead body sounds different from a live one when it falls. I didn't know that till just then. I got out of the car.

I stared at Jordan beneath Morran. "You even have to buy him dinner?" I asked.

"You're a funny fuck," Jordan said. "Look, I just need some help with his pants. I can get out from under him. It's just the pants is all."

"Then get up," I said.

Jordan writhed and bleated about for a time, wriggling out one leg then the other. I watched Morran's head flop to the ground with the hollow thud of a honeydew melon. I untied his shoes. They were nice shoes, not my size, but nice. We slipped the pants off and Jordan changed there in the parking lot.

"No belt," Jordan says. "You believe that? Wears a pair of suspenders with no belt."

"Yeah, that's a real fucking faux-pas, ain't it?" I said. I lugged Morran to the trunk and folded him neatly back inside, next to Jordan's piss-soaked pants.

He came from nowhere: the guy. One minute he was stepping over a parking block, asking us what, *exactly,* we were doing. The next thing I knew, Jordan was back on the ground, his hands over his head, and the guy was staring at my gun while holding his stomach, as if he could put the blood back inside it.

When Jordan's cousin, Aubrey, answered the door, she and Jordan kissed and hugged, then kissed again. They'd always been close, too close. She pecked my cheek, and I said the necessary things. Then I breezed past her towards the kitchen. She took Jordan to the front room.

"I'm *so* glad you guys decided to come," she said.

Jordan said something in an impish voice and Aubrey laughed. Then she popped in through the kitchen's other door as I bumbled through the liquor cabinet. She flipped on the light.

"Here I thought you were going to the bathroom," Aubrey said. "And what are you doing? You're making me look like a bad host."

"Sor-"

"Get your tush out there. What do you want? I'll bring it out to you, hon. Manhattan?"

"Just some scotch," I said.

In the living room, Jordan wouldn't look at me. It was a fragile room. A cabinet in the corner was filled with yellow, Depression-era china. The end tables had glass tops. The lamps were giant bulbs of amber glass that lent the room a warm, comfortable feeling. Everything reflected off the blackened windows. I couldn't see outside. I took a wooden chair and sat up against the wall. When I looked at the front window, I saw the reflection of Jordan looking at me. The phone rang. Aubrey answered.

"How did you know Jordan was here?" I heard her ask. She rounded the corner, standing in the doorway to the living room, the cord wrapped tight around the jamb. She stared hotly at Jordan, who finally stood up and made his way to the hall. She covered the receiver.

"My house is not a meeting room," she hissed. "It's not an *office*. Business isn't conducted here. And here I thought you boys wanted to have a night in with me." She dropped her hands to her side, as though devastated, and started to whimper.

"Aubrey," Jordan said. "Now don't be upset. We'll talk about this when I'm done. Go sit down."

Aubrey slogged over to the davenport where Jordan had been sitting and harrumphed down onto the cushions. Silence strangled the room as she scowled at me.

"What are we having?" I asked.

"What do you care?"

I wanted that scotch just then. Jordan spoke too low for me to hear him. I sat stiff-backed against the wall.

"Tory," Jordan said to me. He held the phone up. "Uncle Phil wants to talk to you."

Phil was not the guy we normally answered to, but I knew he was related to Jordan and that he was more lenient than Frankie Shots.

Aubrey made miffed noises and Jordan joined her on the davenport. I walked into the hall, grabbed the phone, and stared at myself in the window along the front door.

"Yeah?" I said.

"W'happened?"

"Well, this guy spooked us in the parking lot, some Asian guy from the dry cleaning place."

"Fuck you doing at the dry cleaners?"

I lowered my voice: "Jordy pissed himself."

"And you found a dry cleaner open at this hour?"

"Naw, he was changing."

"Changing into what?"

"Morran's pants," I said.

"Who-lly shit." I heard Phil rustling around on the other end. Then he said, "Where's the chink now? The one from the dry cleaners?"

"He's in the trunk with Morran... and the pants."

"Pants?"

"The ones covered in piss."

"Look," Phil said. "All I wanna know is if this going to be a regular problem? This shit with Schnitzel."

"It seems pretty irregular to me," I said.

"I mean occurring at regular intervals, dumbass. Ergo, something I need to worry about."

"I knew exactly what you meant," I said. "And that's my answer."

Phil huffed into the receiver: "What's he doing now?" he asked. "Schnitzel, I mean?"

I rounded the doorjamb and looked over at Jordan. He had his forehead to Aubrey's chin. They were smiling. Aubrey rubbed his arm.

"He's keeping it in the family," I said, turning back around.

"Fuck does that mean, Tory? I'm getting tired of your little comments. I don't have time for this. Tell me what it is you plan to do."

"Where am I supposed to clean out the car? That's all I need to know. It's my problem. I'll fix it."

"Styx," he said. This meant the East River. "And Tory, I think you need to attend to the matter we were talking about."

"This matter being the one we discussed Thursday?"

"The same," he said. "About cleaning out the car. *Thoroughly.*"

"Money," I said.

"No reason for it to be any less."

"I was thinking it'd head in the opposite direction. You know? Up? Like double, that's what I was thinking anyway."

"You got some balls," Phil said. "There's some chink in your trunk I don't give a two squirts of piss about and you want paid for him too. You got some balls, Torrence."

"I don't want to be paid for that," I said. "You know what I want paid for."

"We'll talk about that *after* you clean out the car."

I hung up the phone.

In the living room, Jordan and his cousin looked at me.

"Well, I hope you boys are hungry for ham loaf," Aubrey said.

I snuck a lot of money into my mother's purse the summer after Dad came home in a body bag. She chose to keep working at the factory, not for the money, but simply for something to occupy her mind. So it wasn't like she was strapped for cash. But I'd already started earning my money through frowned-upon means, and I felt the need to do some good with it.

Jordan and I had a plan. It involved a stack of dirty books his father kept in an upstairs closet. Since we were pilfering from his father and storing the stuff in his garage, I was the one who did all the dirty work while Jordan distracted whoever might be in the house. I removed pages instead of stealing the whole book. I'd find the less attractive, skinny pinup girls who weren't at the center. They were still lookers, like any girl in one of those books, but they were pictures Jordan's father would never notice were gone. And I cut them close to the binding with a jackknife my dad gave me, stashing the the girls in my goulashes rather than my pockets. They were safer there.

Our "theater" was in the rafters of his parents' garage. Unlike my mother and I, the Profacis lived in a house that had been in their family for decades. It had a tall, detached garage with old planks of wood stored up in the rafters. In back, there was a concealed corner with a small circular window that let in dusty light. Once a week we'd take a group of three or four kids up there. They'd pay their quarter, then we'd all climb the tool bench and slink through the rafters to the spot where Jordan had pinned the girls to the wall and hung a bed sheet over them. They were beautiful, those girls: the once black-and-white pictures professionally colored in to give their arms and thighs that rounded, pink hue. I envied the man who earned his living coloring in a woman's areolae.

Jay Dotts was a perverted kid who came to the garage every week, no matter if we'd changed out some of the pictures or not. He'd wait in the alley near some garbage cans until we emerged from the house and headed for the garage. Then he followed us inside and up into the sooty rafters.

"How much for the girl holding those coconuts?" he asked one day, after Jordan had thrown back the curtain.

"They're not for sale," Jordan said.

"Everything is for sale," I said.

Jordan looked at me, stunned. We'd never talked about this before, but in all honesty I was surprised it had taken this long for someone to ask.

"I'll give you a dime," Jay said.

"Nothing's for sale for that price," I said. I ripped the bed-sheet from Jordan's hand, pulling it over the pictures.

"Wait!" Jay said. "Dime and a half."

"That girl's been up there for weeks," I said. "You had your eye on her ever since you first came. Fifty cents."

He dug through his pocket and produced some lint and loose change. "I got a quarter and..." He looked at his hand, counting the change, "...seven cents."

I grabbed the change, then unpinned the girl from the plaster wall and handed it to him. "But you owe forty cents if you want in next week," I said.

He didn't say anything. He grabbed the page from me and stared at it, awestruck. Jordan pulled the curtain back over the pictures once again. He looked at Jay uncomfortably, unsure what to make of this situation.

We all headed for the front of the garage: Jay leading the way, then Jordan, and I followed. That's when Jordan just disappeared. One minute, I heard him say something to Jay about a girl at school, and the next thing I knew I was staring at a plume of glittering dust. He'd stepped somewhere wrong, a place with little or nothing to hold him. When he landed, he screamed in a way boys were never supposed to, letting go his pre-pubescent pitch—something we all hid at that age. Jay and I both looked down the hole he'd fallen through; there laid Jordan on the collapsed roof of his father's Plymouth, the windows busted out, the horn was blaring from part of the roof pressing against it. And Jordan began to scream.

Jay and I couldn't get down fast enough. We knocked our heads and knees on every joist trying to find a different way down than the one Jordan had taken. Just as we reached the ground, Jordan's father burst through the door. That's when Jay crammed the girlie picture into his mouth. Mr. Profaci rushed over to the car, running his good hand through his hair.

"What happened? What happened?" He stood over Jordan, touching his boy lightly. Jordan rolled back and forth unable to speak, the roof of the car crinkling under his weight. His face was a pathetic painting of dust and tears.

Mr. Profaci turned to Jay and me. "Tell me what happened!"

"Jordan fell from the rafters," I said. Jay sidled behind me, his mouth full of paper.

Jordan's father turned to his son briefly. He looked up at the spot above the car, then he rushed for the door.

"Ma!" he screamed out in the daylight. "Ma! Call an ambulance! Jordan's hurt hisself." He came back into the garage. "What were you doing up there?" he asked me.

And of course I couldn't tell him, but I had that foolproof, utilitarian excuse all children have and, unfortunately (at a certain age) lose:

"We were playing," I said.

He looked past me, at Jay, and pointed his finger at him.

"Who are you?" he demanded. "What are you doing here?"

All his questions seemed unimportant and irrelevant given the circumstance, but he goaded Jay once again, nudging me out of the way.

"What's in your mouth?" he asked, poking the boy in the chest. He held his good hand up to Jay's chin. Jay opened his mouth slowly, as though yawning, and tongued the wadded picture into Mr. Profaci's hand. It took Mr. Profaci some time to get the picture unwrinkled. The paper was wet and he could barely hold it with his bum arm. But he finally got it, and when he did, he stared at a smiling woman holding two coconuts and wearing nothing but a lei.

I pulled the car as close to the Whitestone as I could get it. The less we had to carry Morran and the dry-cleaner through Ferry Point Park, the better. Queens winked its eyes at us from across the river, a wall of soft blues and oranges disappearing down the coast. I opened the door and saw my breath for the first time that year. The East River would be freezing. I opened the trunk. It smelled like hot rain in there. We loaded up our shoulders: me with Morran, Jordan with the dry cleaner. For a while Jordan whistled a Christmas carol, something like "Little Drummer Boy," but then the Asian got heavy on him.

"Tory, come on. I need a break," he said.

"We're almost there."

"Naw, I can't go. I'll catch up with you."

"Don't stop," I said. "Someone spooks me again, you'll be carrying two to the river instead of one."

But then Jordan fell. He tripped over a tree root, dropped the Asian, and shot forward, bumping into me and Morran. Instead of falling, I dropped Morran and grabbed Jordan around the neck in a playful headlock. He started laughing, really laughing, from deep in his gut. We bumbled through the park together, the black trees towering over us. He got turned around in my grip somehow and tried grabbing my legs to take me down, but I was back-stepping too fast for him, all the while heading us towards the river, until I felt the soft banks squelch beneath my boots. That's when I threw Jordan sideways into the water, soaking both of us instantly. One minute dry, the next minute wet: that was my life.

"Torrence!" he gurgled. "Torrence, what the hell are you...do-ing?"

His hands clenched my arms as I forced his head underwater. He kicked his feet in a frenzy. White bubbles burbled up near my face. Soon, his hands went rigid, like two garden trowels around my wrist. They slipped into the dark water with the rest of him. I stood up and stared at the darkened park, the sound of the river suddenly loud around me. I cleared my throat. I went back for the others.

Jeremy Schnee

Unseen

Imagine yourself invisible. Scientific experiment gone awry, foolish attempt at magic, perhaps a fluke of luck—a lightning strike bending the color spectrum around you. The beginning doesn't matter so much. At least, not as much as the possibilities this new perspective can offer.

Before anything else, indulge. A goose-bumped bank teller asking clients if they hear breathing will be none the wiser when the money drawer empties. Jewelry does; however, fit easier in a mouth or fist, assuming clothes would hinder here. Just be sure not to wander into vaults that might close for days on end. Speaking of wandering, locker rooms surely come to mind. As do dressing rooms, saunas, the home of someone beautiful. Be careful. A shadow in shower's mist, an accidental groan, footprints in mud outside a bedroom window, these are all bound to scare someone. Yet hopefully such amusements will inspire your true understanding of the word, anywhere.

"Restricted to the public," no longer applies. Cross chained off areas in museums, go in backrooms at restaurants. Go through drawers of a seemingly perfect, not-so-friendly-friend (bring dog treats as necessary). Visit the secret side of the world, or in secret, visit the world. Avoid airport security; find empty seats on planes; travel in style, sneaking meals and hotel keys.

At some point the honeymoon period will grow tiresome. The ease with which you can steal dulls thrill. As for staring at naked people who think they're alone, not all sights, sounds, and smells are pleasant. Dodging crowds is stressful and travel is potentially dangerous. Yelling for help from a collapsed floor in a restricted area—no wonder it was chained off—is no way to debut your invisible self. Eventually you are going to wish to return to some aspect of your old life. This is the first option not open to you.

No reversing the invisibility, your best bet is comfortable clothing and a hat, always a hat. Be warned of make-up. Even painted like a mannequin, the gaping voids left in your eyes and mouth are especially startling. If in a relationship and fainting seems possible, forget clothes and tell the significant other with arms ready. They may poke, prod, faint again. If they don't run, try and salvage something. Cook dinner, watch movies and well, sex with an invisible partner should be kinky if not a bit awkward. Then leave home. Arm outstretched, seeming to hold air, their palms will sweat. When nuzzled by what appears to be floating laundry, their arms and legs will fidget. When ordering food and buying tickets, their voices will crack, but mostly in facing the public, watch their eyes. Watch them avert further and further away.

For those married, maybe with nigh-unbreakable bonds; maybe with kids, consider what you have left to offer: media attention and whispers, jokes around school or the workplace that make them uncomfortable, resentful. Or perhaps what you can offer is a void in the family photo, the one in which they gather around and where your face and hands should be, there's only background blue.

Speaking of family, use a phone to tell worrisome parents. Maybe its best letting brothers and sisters remember how you once were. In this transition, friends might be a net to fall on, but be wary of those excited by your new-found gift/curse. "Favors," will only encourage exploitation. In other cases, gossip will be plentiful and though distance isn't the same as invisibility, some friends will disappear.

Perhaps the job can lend some comfort. If it's customer service, teaching, or door to door sales, don't bother. Construction, warehousing, anything minutely dangerous is worse. The inanimate tends to blend. A yellow vest floating along the edge of a highway, perched atop a ladder, under dropping tools, is asking for a gruesome end. Considering hazards, a city of crosswalks isn't exactly inviting. Perhaps neither is a small town: one where kids spy on you and anytime something goes missing, your house is the first pointed to.

Yet stripped of obligation, there is opportunity. Live anywhere. A clement climate is favorable if occasional naked walks sound appealing. Slow-moving traffic is a definite plus. You'll certainly need something to do for a living (especially if guilt over stolen goods caused you to give them back). Internet work is a cop-out. Appearances on TV, movie special effects, the circus angle, are all too obvious.

How about a taxi service where the car drives itself, or seems to? For the homebody, consider a haunted bed and breakfast? Creepy whispers, echoing footsteps, doors that slam at night, all provided with plates of eggs and bacon that float to the table by morning. A prank service could be lucrative. Stiff leashes that look like an invisible dog walking have nothing on you. A private investigation firm would have clients lining up at the door for you. Just know that there are opportunities.

The same might be true with people. Impossible to entirely vanish, parents or siblings might not care. They've seen plenty enough to remember you anyhow. Plus, you're perfect for their surprise-parties. Friends who want to grab a drink and listen to how this all began, who say you tell damnedest of stories, aren't going anywhere. Your children might not see a void in that photo either, not translucent space, but someone they always know where to find.

Of course in some cases people will need to come anew, and some gaps may never be filled. In the luckiest of instances though, lovers, who despite your insistences won't let you leave, or who discover you regardless of invisibility. Lovers who scoff at stares on the street, who sit intent when you speak, who cuddle to the embrace when the bed dips opposite, well for certain, don't hold back in showing them all you can offer. And if people such as this exist, don't only let them see you, open your own eyes. Open them wide.

William Peskett

Snake Eyes

Coming up to fifty and he'd torn down all the straights and cornered most of the bends just like it said in the manual. Three children, the best he could have hoped for, were at university in England, or would be by next year. He'd made regional-level director in his company, which was more than he'd ever considered his goal. And he'd ditched only one wife along the way. It could have been more, he realized, as he had no illusions that he was an easy man to live with. Knowing the truth of that, after the split he'd dedicated himself to his work and to his painting, rather than to filling the emptiness he'd created in his own life.

The posting to South-East Asia had changed the dynamics of his life. The old void his earlier divorce had left was filled within a year by a simple country girl who knew how to please her man. She came with two kids of her own, now nearly grown up, so there seemed no need to make more babies.

That was eight years ago now, and while his newish wife was still around and still knew how to cook a spectacular masaman curry, the intimacy that had driven him to her when they first met was now, while not non-existent, at best sporadic.

It seemed to suit them both. He had no desire to augment the physical love he shared with his wife by accepting any of the many commercial offers that living and working in Bangkok frequently presented to him. Nor was he attracted by any of the bustling women he encountered at management level in his company. He was reaching that age, he sometimes thought, when it became necessary to make use of the word 'libido'. The depressing thing he learnt was that it was a word you only needed to describe something that was in decline.

A year or so previously, he had discovered—or rather rediscovered—the easy satisfaction of composing his own pleasure. It was ridiculous to think of it as a revelation, since the simple equipment and knowledge of its workings that now gave him such enjoyable sensations had been with him all his life. Rather, he thought of it as a re-evaluation of a pre-condition, a second chance to experience joy from a situation that was, basically, nothing new.

He first began on this new journey in bed. He would lie awake at night, unable to sleep perhaps because of a niggling worry that he'd left some piece of work undone, or because he was running through the possible dynamics of a meeting that he'd have to attend the next day. His wife would be lying next to him, quiet and still. If she was asleep or awake he couldn't tell; she didn't snore.

At first, it was merely something to hold onto, like a comforter. He would cradle it in his right hand and feel its relaxed, compliant bulk, like a long balloon of warm water, perhaps, or a raw sausage or some item of uncooked pastry. What did a spring roll feel like before it was fried? He had no idea. But the difference between all these comparators and the real thing was that the real thing felt so good. It was not only good to hold (the sensations that came to him through his palm and fingers) but good to be held (the sensations that came directly from his penis).

On nights when it was clear his wife didn't want to make love— and those were frequent—the pattern was repeated; he would clasp and caress his penis softly until sleep came. This was all he needed; this was all his libido demanded. Every boy did a lot more, he was sure; his behaviour was nothing that caused him any anxiety.

But it became more serious. At work, he would sometimes find that, while walking along the corridor or passing between the desks of his subordinates with his hand casually pushed into his trouser pocket, he would make glancing contact with his penis and enjoy a frisson of forbidden pleasure.

One weekend when his wife had gone to the market and left him sitting on the secluded balcony of their condominium with a pot of coffee and the *Bangkok Post,* on impulse he unzipped his fly and pulled his penis half into view. He stared at it for some time before coming to a new realization: it was beautiful. Until now, he hadn't appreciated what a handsome organ it was—structured yet amorphous, soft yet powerful. He longed to make it the subject of a painting and wondered how he could abstract its essence sufficiently so as not to alarm his wife. He would hang the picture in their drawing room and call it something like *Insight 3.*

It looked back at him blankly, its vertical slot of a mouth seeming to express shock or surprise, but of a very familiar kind. This was his penis after all; they'd come through alot together. He'd shot the DNA to make three kids through that fulsomely-lipped mouth, he mused philosophically, plus a lot more that had gone nowhere in a genetic sense. And he hardly wanted to think about the beer he'd pissed through it. And the wine. And the rest.

He smiled at his cock and, with help, it smiled back, though the expression was awkward as its head was upside-down, like the smile of a limbo dancer. If he twisted the whole thing around, he found he could confront it properly, face to face and the right way up. The little puffy cheeks below its mouth bulged like jowls; above was the high, noble forehead; and behind that rolled the comfortable ruff of prepuce, like the neck of a fisherman's favourite old sweater.

One negative he considered was that it was blind, and this insight suddenly made him think of his cock as a massive underground grub, pasty pink and etiolated because it had never been allowed access to the light. If only there were eyes in that wide flat head, he mused. If only their communication could be more than blind and he could express his gratitude for the pleasure his penis gave to him. That would bring perfection to the joy of their blossoming relationship.

His new hobby was getting more serious. In bed now he would continue his rhythmic stroking until his penis was fully engorged. He found he could achieve this with the minimum of movement, and thus not risk waking his wife. One thumb twitching behind the head for a few minutes was all that was required to extend the organ across his thigh. He would maintain this state of tumescence for five minutes or so before replacing the foreskin and relaxing into sleep.

He took a pair of his weekend shorts and unpicked the stitching in one pocket. If his wife had noticed, she would have put the damage down to understandable wear and tear, but in reality, he used the aperture to reach through and caress his penis while in the most public places. Accompanying his wife to the supermarket, for example, was an ideal opportunity to bring it to life. Bored by the purchase of groceries, he would stroll among the displays of fruit and vegetables, both hands in his pockets, with one coaxing his penis to erection. He would jingle the keys in his left pocket to disguise any movement that might be required to create exquisite pleasure in the right.

He began to worry that his interest in his penis had become an obsession. But what if it had? Was it an obsession that was causing anyone harm? Was it anything that could escalate into evil behaviour? He thought not. Was he obtaining satisfaction from his own caresses that should have been provided by his wife? Possibly. This did cause him some pause for thought. But his wife and he did still make love, and the extent of this seemed to be all that his wife required, so his feelings of guilt were quickly assuaged. Without guilt, he became more honest about his own feelings; he had to admit it, he had fallen in love with his penis.

He quickly assured himself that this wasn't an exclusive love. He still loved his wife of course; he loved his three children naturally. This was a love that he could indulge in addition to these human relationships, despite its special nature. There was no denying the singular bond that existed between a man and his penis.

One Saturday, his wife suggested making a trip to the zoo. It was somewhere they'd been before, but not often. It was a huge place, and included a pleasant park in which they could stroll while observing the animals. He'd been entertaining clients the night before and so considered that the walk and the fresh air would help clear the residue of unmetabolized alcohol still in his blood.

So together they walked and chatted and enjoyed the plants and animals until they reached the reptile house. Inside, down the steps, it was dark and hot. The smell of the scaly inhabitants was musty and close. He gripped the wall beside a glass window to catch his breath and stared at a python on a branch beyond the barrier. The snake didn't move except for an occasional flick of its tongue. Its neck lay along the branch, long and thick. Its bulbous head extended beyond the end of the branch, held up by the stiffness of its neck.

The heat was becoming too much. The eyes in the snake's smooth high forehead stared. In a flash it came to him that the lack of air in the reptile house was stifling him and before he could leave the building he realized he had something very important to do.

The next week he told his personal assistant he'd be gone from the office for the afternoon and instructed his driver to take him to a large Bangkok hospital. It was one his wife and he used regularly for minor matters. In the back of the car, he was pleased to note that a large hole had appeared in the right pocket of his work trousers. As the car jerked through the heavy Bangkok traffic, he took comfort from his own gentle caresses.

At the hospital he located the cosmetic surgery department and told the receptionist that he wanted to speak to a doctor about an elective procedure. After a short wait, he was ushered into a small consultation room and soon joined by a doctor.

'How can I help you?' she asked.

'I would like to have a small operation, nothing very serious.'

'I see. What operation would you like?' She had a notepad in front of her and twiddled a pen in her fingers but so far the doctor had written nothing.

'It's to do with my penis,' he said, quite calmly and without a hint of embarrassment.

'I see. Is it to increase the length? The girth? What exactly would you like us to do?' The woman was very attractive. He very much liked to hear her talking about him in that way.

'No, it's not the length, and it's not the girth. Both of those dimensions are quite satisfactory,' he smirked, then worried that he may have given it a little too much swagger. However, the doctor showed no reaction.

'Then what?' she asked.

'I would like you to insert…to give it some eyes,' he said quickly.

'Eyes? I see.' The doctor faltered momentarily, but swallowed and continued. 'May I ask why?'

'So it can see.'

'I see.'

'Yes.'

'Why do you want it to see?'

'I want our relationship—between my penis and myself, you understand—to be more equal. We are very much in love. We give each other physical pleasure of course, but I want to extend that to make it more…'

'Sharing?'

'Yes, sharing's a good word.'

'And companionable?'

'Yes. Thank you for your understanding.'

'But that's my job! What you're asking for is a penile ocular transplant, what we surgeons call a POT. Actually, we don't get so much demand for this procedure. I shall have to consult with colleagues. Please excuse me for a moment.'

With that, the doctor left the room. He sat at the doctor's desk and waited. On the wall was a poster showing two women, one with small breasts, the other with large breasts; when he finally looked at her face he realised they were the same woman. On the desk was the doctor's notepad, still blank.

After some time, the doctor returned and said: 'Yes, we can do as you wish, we can perform a POT. But we do have a small problem.'

'What's the problem?' he asked.

'It's getting the right donor. People commonly donate their eyes for transplantation after their death, but this is normally restricted to facial use. Obtaining authorisation for penile transplantation is very rare. There could be a long wait. I'm sorry.'

'I don't want people's eyes,' he replied. 'They would be much too big and very scary. It would be very weird thinking about who had owned them—and looked through them—before. No, I want something a lot smaller than that, something alert yet loving, like a snake.'

'Oh, I see. I'm sorry I misunderstood. Then it seems we do not have that problem. Finding a suitable snake donor is much easier than locating a human one for the simple reason that the snake has no choice. Ha ha,' the doctor laughed quickly. 'Please excuse me for a moment.'

After a short while, the doctor returned with some papers. 'You're all booked in. The procedure will cost 430,000 baht. Please sign here and if I could have your credit card?'

He signed the document and handed over his card, which the doctor took out of the room. She returned again with the slip, which he signed.

'If you would now please undress and lie on the bed,' she directed, while snapping on some rubber gloves.

He lay naked on the small examination couch as the doctor approached with a hypodermic syringe.

'You have the snake?' he asked as she pierced his skin.

'Just leave all the arrangements to us,' she replied, soothingly.

When he awoke, he was still in the same room. He lifted his head slowly and was surprised to find his wife sitting by the side of the bed. He was confused.

'Did it go alright?' he asked.

'Did what go alright?' his wife replied.

'The…thing. You know. No, sorry. Actually, why am I here?'

'You passed out.'

'I know, but…what? When did I pass out?'

'About two hours ago. You fainted at the zoo. You hit your head on the step.'

He put his hand to his head and felt the bandage. Glancing down, he noticed he was still wearing his shorts. He put his hand in his pocket. It felt too normal. He couldn't find the sort of post-operative wrappings he'd expected.

'Come on, sit up,' his wife encouraged. 'How do you feel?'

'Kind of weak,' he replied.

He sat on the edge of the bed for some minutes and drank half a glass of water before deciding that he wanted to leave: 'Come on, let's go home.'

'If you feel better.'

'Yes, I'm fine.'

'I'll just go and pay.'

'I've already…'

'How could you have done?'

'No, right. You go and pay, sorry.'

He felt a little dizzy as he got up and walked slowly from the consultation room, a confusion that increased as he emerged through the front doors of the building and realized that he was leaving quite a different hospital from the one he'd entered.

'I've got my driver here,' he said weakly, wondering really if it was true.

'No you haven't, darling, it's Saturday. We're using my car.'

VISUAL ART

Brian Forrest
Berlin in the 1020s: Show Girls 3
Ink on paper
12" x 9"

Adam Roberts

Oliver Hardy

Digital Painting, 13.52" x 15.8".

Vinoth Rajendran

Gorgon

Pen and marker on paper, 8.3" x 11.7".

Vinoth Rajendran

Witch Doctor

Pen and marker on paper, 8.3" x 11.7".

Kendall James

Spruce Tree House, Mesa Verde, Co.

Photography, 2013.

Rhiannon James

Borderlands 2

Digital manipulation of an acrylic painting, 16" x 22".

Rhiannon James

Yolandi I

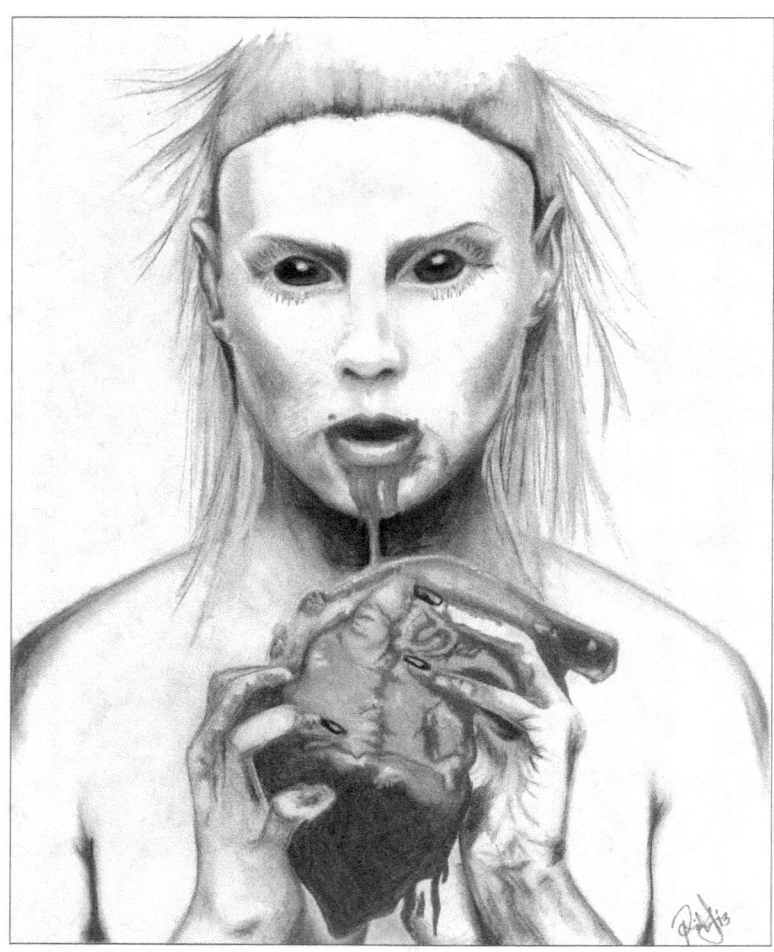

Mixed media with charcoal, prisma color, and acrylic, 16" x 22".

Rhiannon James

Yolandi II

Acrylic, 11" x 22".

SPECIAL SECTION

Brian Forrest
Berlin in the 1020s: Make-up
Ink on paper
12" x 9"

Foreword

By combining tangible data and emerging technologies, University of Central Oklahoma students researched and developed multimedia compositions during the Fall 2013 semester.

The creative scholarship featured in this section demonstrates the power and profundity of stereotypes. Some students elected to focus on common misconceptions whereas others chose to concentrate on tangential fallacies. In each instance, their contributions enhance our understanding of contemporary realities. Mvto.

Dr. Timothy Petete

37% [of those surveyed] said they consider "feminist" to be a negative term, compared to only 26% who consider it a positive term.

(29% said it's a neutral term.)

Merriam-Webster Dictionary defines feminism as

"the theory of the political, economic, and social equality of the sexes."

Men were also more likely than women to consider "feminist" a negative term (32% to 42%), but even among women, more said the term is negative than positive (29% to 32 %).

Trevor Larson

How Society Sees
Mental Illness

She's dangerous.

Worthless.

I'm afraid of her.

She's crazy.

Keep her away from me.

She hears voices.

Deranged.

Welfare

Perception

Why is there such a negative connotation about welfare?

"The Welfare Queen" stereotype originated with Ronald Regan during his presidential campaign, where he spoke of a woman with a Cadillac and jewels who paid for food with food stamps.

- "Welfare Queen"
- "They only have kids to get more money."
- "They choose not to work, and I pay for it!"
- "If they would just pull themselves up by their bootstraps…"
- "She is on welfare and drives a better car than I do."
- "I'm funding their drug habits."
- "They get free iPhones."
- "They game the system."

Reality

- 91% of people on welfare are elderly, disabled, or live in working households.*
- Cycles of joblessness are created by societal conditions.
- Drug testing of welfare recipients has not proven to be successful, and states that have instituted this policy have lost excessive amounts of money.*
- People who stay on welfare normally cannot get jobs because they don't have telephones or vehicles, and welfare does not pay enough to cover these items.

*Sources

- http://www.cbpp.org/cms/?fa=view&id=3677
- http://www.salon.com/2013/08/29/gop's_inane_money_eating_sham_drug_tests_for_welfare_a_huge_failure/

Depression

HEY GUYS,
I THINK I MIGHT BE
DEPRESSED.

"No, you just have
a bad case of the **blues**."

"What do you have
to be depressed about?
A lot of people have worse
problems than you."

"Even if you are feeling
depressed, it's not like you
have an illness. Don't worry,
you will snap out of it."

I KNOW
SOMETHING IS
NOT RIGHT, BUT I
CAN'T REALLY
EXPLAIN IT.

"Your mood doesn't
affect your body."

"Depression doesn't
cause physical pain,
you are probably
just stressed."

"People have aches and
pains all of the time, don't
be such a drama queen."

"Depression is all in
your head; it's not a real
disease or illness."

I FEEL
ANXIOUS AND
TENSE, BUT I DON'T
WANT TO WORRY ANYONE
SO I WON'T SAY
ANYTHING.

"Everything seems
normal, so there is no
reason to ask if he
is doing ok."

"You look fine,
so there is nothing
to worry about."

If there was
something wrong
he would say something,
so everything must be fine
because he looks ok."

I KNOW SOMETHING IS NOT RIGHT, BUT I CAN'T REALLY EXPLAIN IT.

"If you were depressed you would be able to explain how you feel."

"If you can't explain it then you aren't depressed, because you have to talk about how you feel to get better."

"People who are depressed know exactly how they feel; you're just confused because you don't feel like you normally do."

I DON'T LOOK LIKE A NORMAL DEPRESSED PERSON; I AM JUST TIRED OR STRESSED OUT.

"Women get depressed, not men."

"Stress and fatigue are common in people with depression."

"Depression is not a bias, it does not care about your gender, race, or culture; it can affect anyone."

"Depression is an illness, people can't just snap out of it. If not treated, depression can be deadly."

Will you help me? | Thanks! But I've got it.

I can't do it. | I can do it.

Will you push me? | I'll push myself.

People with disabilities always need help. | Many people with disabilities are independent and can accomplish most things by themselves.

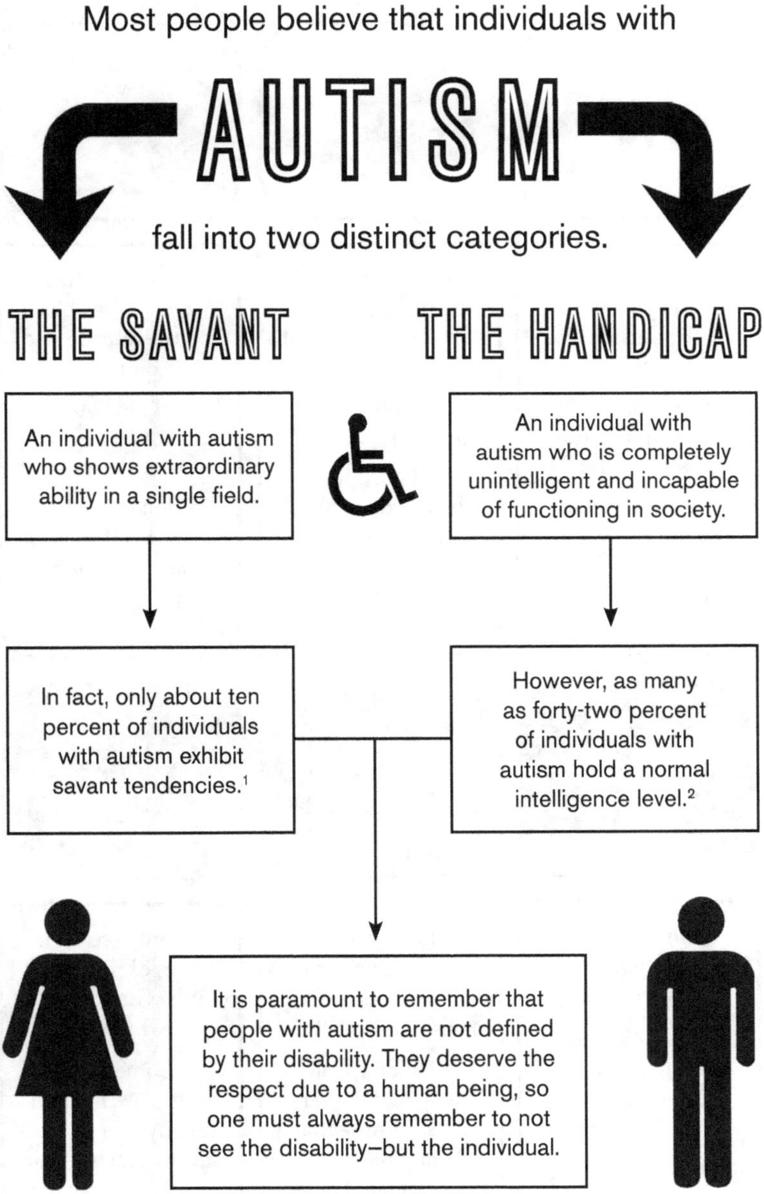

Most people believe that individuals with

fall into two distinct categories.

THE SAVANT

THE HANDICAP

An individual with autism who shows extraordinary ability in a single field.

An individual with autism who is completely unintelligent and incapable of functioning in society.

In fact, only about ten percent of individuals with autism exhibit savant tendencies.[1]

However, as many as forty-two percent of individuals with autism hold a normal intelligence level.[2]

It is paramount to remember that people with autism are not defined by their disability. They deserve the respect due to a human being, so one must always remember to not see the disability—but the individual.

1 Bazelon, Emily. "What Autistic Girls Are Made Of." *The New York Times Magazine.* The New York Times, 5 Aug. 2007. Web. 24 Sept. 2013. <http://www.nytimes.com/2007/08/05/magazine/05autism-t.html>

2 Treffort, Darold. "The Savant Syndrome: Islands of Genius." *Autism Today.* Autism Today, n.d. Web. 24 Sept. 2013. <http://www.autismtoday.com/articles/SavantSyndrome.htm>

"Oh no, here comes banana girl, yellow on the outside and white on the inside!"

"She thinks that she is smarter than everyone else."

"Where is she from? It doesn't matter, they all look alike anyway."

"Apples remind me of Indians, red on the outside and white on the inside."

"He probably lives on a reservation."

"Poor kid, he has no future. He will probably be an alcoholic or commit suicide."

"Ha ha, he is like an Oreo cookie, black on the outside and white on the inside."

"Do you think he ever washes his hair?"

"I don't care how light his skin is or what color his eyes are, he is black!"

"I am a unique individual with my own goals."

"If I have trouble making friends at school, I remind myself to relax and be myself."

"I am Chinese American."

"I have a bright future ahead of me that is filled with possibility."

"When I feel bullied by other kids, I know that I can talk to my friends and family."

"I am proud of my Native American heritage."

"I embrace both sides of my race, it is what makes me different."

"Sometimes kids tease me and say my hair stinks, but I wash my hair just like everyone else does."

"I am bi-racial."

- "They're all drug addicts."
- "They're mentally ill."
- "They're lying to get your money."
- "Support system gave up."
- "No ambition."
- "They did this to themselves."
- http://www.nationalhomelessness.org/factsheets/ Mental_Illness.html
- http://www.endhomelessness.org/library/entry/ the-state-of-homelessness-in-america-2012

"Being a stay-at-home mom
is easy because you don't have
to do any hard work."

"Women are happier and want
to be stay-at-home moms."

"Stay-at-home moms don't
need to work because their
husbands make enough
money to support them."

"Women are happy to
help financially provide
for their families."

"A stay-at-home mom
works hard. She does all the
housework, cooking, laundry,
and often takes care of the
kids by herself."

"A mom may be a stay-at-
home mom because she
cannot afford to pay for
childcare, even
while working."

"Being a stay-at-home
mom can be stressful work."

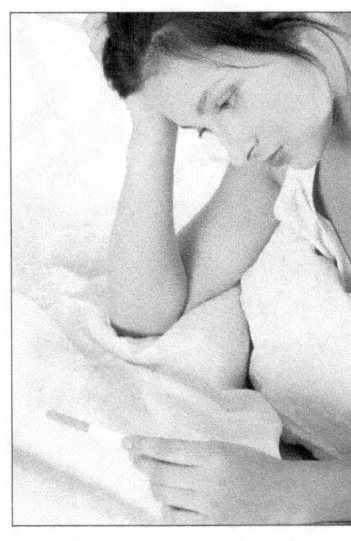

"She is promiscuous."

"Mmhmm…"

"Her life is over."

"Her relationship with the father won't last."

"She will work minimum wage jobs for the rest of her life."

"I graduated high school, worked my way up in my job, and now I'm manager."

"My child's father and I have been married for twenty years."

"I furthered my education."

"My child is the greatest thing that ever happened to me."

Not all teen moms are the same.

Sources:

http://www.loop21.com/life/sex-uneducated-why-teens-think-they-cant-get-pregnant

http://www.practicenotes.org/vol1_no1/teen_pregnancy_and_parenting.htm

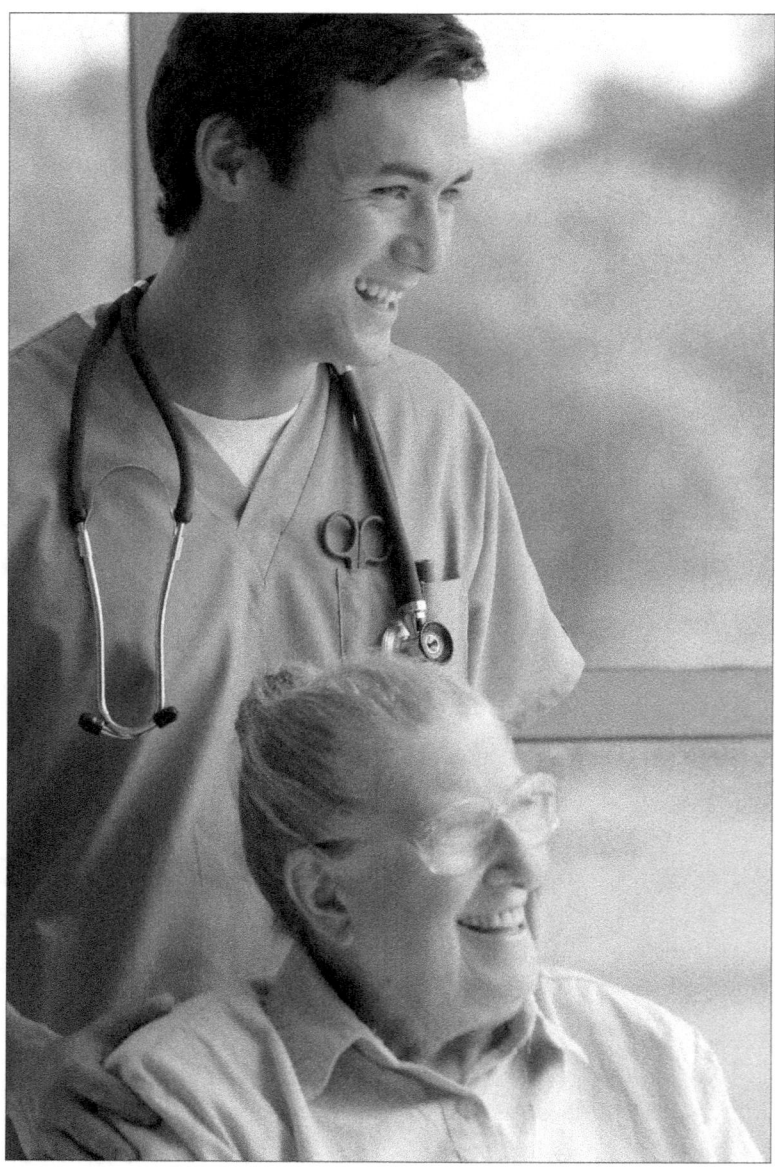

According to a U.S. Census Bureau study, Newsroom reports that the proportion of male nurses has more than tripled since 1970 from 2.7% to 9.6%.

NONFICTION

Brian Forrest
Berlin in the 1020s: Dancers 1
Ink on paper
12" x 9"

Francis DiClemente

The Defiled Ice Cream Cone

Before my family moved to a rural stretch of land in south Rome, New York, in the late 1970s, we lived in a duplex at 126 Stanwix Street in the heart of the city, a block away from the Oneida County Courthouse, a red brick building with white columns and a dome top. Stanwix Street connects two of Rome's main thoroughfares: Black River Boulevard and James Street. And the neighborhood's appeal was limited to its proximity to downtown, the post office, city hall, gas stations, and stores; otherwise, it offered residents a rough, neglected setting where potholes often went unfilled and you could find smashed beer bottles and other trash scattered on the sidewalks following summer weekends.

Our house, much like the neighborhood, needed some work. The unstable porch steps creaked whenever someone walked on them, the white paint and emerald trim were cracked, and the whole structure seemed to tilt slightly to the left.

But the house did have a working washer and dryer in the cellar and a sewing machine for my mother, and Dad could grow tomato plants in a small garden area on our property near a sloping chain-link fence.

I spent hours tossing a basketball toward the rusted, net-less hoop already attached to the garage, and turned the small backyard into my personal Wiffle ball domain. My sister and I could also play on a swing set in the backyard, and I remember picking dandelions when they popped up on the lawn in the spring after the blanket of winter snow receded.

Linda and Robbie Blackwood (names changed) lived across the street in an apartment building covered with cedar shake shingles. The building was often ensconced in shade, and I remember Linda and Robbie spending a lot of time at our house. They were poor, and their mother may have been on welfare. They wore frayed clothes, and I heard other people refer to them as "wellies."

But their financial situation had no bearing on our friendship; they lived nearby, and we just had fun playing together.

Linda and I were about the same age. She was short and wiry and had blond hair. As an athlete, she could rival any boy in the neighborhood. She could beat me from home plate to first base in a sprint, and her mix of fastballs and off-speed pitches usually left me dizzy in the backyard batter's box.

I think Robbie was older than Linda, but only by a year or two; he was stocky and also had blond hair. I don't think I ever saw their mother, not even once, but she would often yell at Robbie and Linda from her window and tell them to "get their asses inside."

Robbie and Linda never mentioned their father, but it seemed like he was away and may have left them. They did not discuss his absence from their lives, so I did not ask them about it. But I always wondered if he would show up one day. Or was he already dead?

Routine ruled our summer months. In the mornings, after breakfast, Linda and Robbie would stop at my house. We would run through the neighborhood, exploring whatever caught our attention. We would build forts, jump rope, play hopscotch or hide-and-seek, shoot hoops, and play kickball or Wiffle ball.

I also remember digging for musket balls and arrows in a plot of land near the site of Fort Stanwix, which had been reconstructed as a national monument in Rome. We had learned in school that many historians considered the siege of Fort Stanwix a turning point in the Revolutionary War because the Continental Army, under the command of Colonel Peter Gansevoort, repelled a lengthy British assault led by General Barry St. Leger and thus helped to thwart a three-pronged plan by the British to divide the colonies.

But we didn't care about the historical significance of Fort Stanwix; we just wanted to find some artifacts that we could trade with each other or use in our "war games."

We would eat lunch, separately, and then meet again in early afternoon and play Wiffle ball or some other game the rest of the day, taking brief breaks to chug a few glasses of cherry or grape Kool-Aid, which I would grab from inside the house. And it seemed like Robbie never washed off the red or purple Kool-Aid stain that circled his mouth the entire summer.

We would split up at about five in the afternoon, as Mrs. Blackwood made her kids eat an early supper at a fast food restaurant. Throughout the summer months they rotated between McDonald's, Burger King, Dairy Queen, Kentucky Fried Chicken and other fast food spots in Rome.

Linda said her mom refused to cook in the summer because their apartment lacked air conditioning. I was envious of their diet of burgers, chicken, fries and shakes, and I asked my mom why we couldn't eat out every night like the Blackwoods. She gave me some explanation about the importance of home-cooked meals, but as a kid, I didn't understand her reasoning.

Dad would come home from his job at the Sears store at about 6:15 p.m. every weekday, and I would shovel down whatever Mom placed on my plate before excusing myself and racing out to meet Linda and Robbie for a few games of kickball or hide-and-seek before I had to come inside for the night.

But one July day our playtime schedule was altered by a selfish act I would regret for years to come. The Blackwoods had returned home from their fast food dinner, and Linda and Robbie were playing outside. I was inside the house at the time, most likely watching "The Electric Company" or another PBS show, when I heard the sound of the ice cream truck luring me away from the television.

"Not before dinner," Mom said after I jumped out of the reclining chair and begged her for money.

"Please Mom, just a small twist cone."

"I said no."

I threw my arms up in protest and ran to the window. I focused my gaze on the "Ice Cream Man" as he distributed the frozen treats at the curb. Clad in his clean, white uniform, he appeared like a modern-day knight, rushing to the succor of the Stanwix Street children, bringing cooling relief to the kids and quenching the heat that rose from the asphalt.

"Mom, I'll be outside until Dad gets home."

"Stay inside the yard," she hollered from the kitchen.

"OK," I said on my way out the door.

I pushed open the screen door and let it slam behind me, and the porch groaned as I leapt off the top step. Linda and Robbie were standing on the other side of the chain-link fence that separated our backyard from an adjacent lot. They were both holding ice cream cones, and they were licking them quickly because the sun was still bright and the heat was melting the ice cream.

I walked up to my side of the fence, and Linda came toward me on the other side.

"We got ice cream," Linda said.

"Yeah," I said.

Robbie followed his sister and approached the fence. His flavor was chocolate, and I noticed a trickle of brown liquid rolling down his forearm. He then started taunting me because he had ice cream and I did not.

I have replayed this incident in my head more times than I would like to admit. And no matter how much I want to, I can't stop myself, or more accurately, the memory of myself, from doing what I did that day.

"You want a lick?" Robbie asked me.

"Sure," I said, my eyes fixed on his cone.

I think Linda may have told her brother they needed to get home before their ice cream melted. But Robbie ignored her. Instead, he extended his arm and held the cone over the top of the fence. He may have said something like, "Here, try it."

Yet when I reached up to take the cone, he yanked it away and I clutched a handful of air.

"Madge ya [Made you] look, now suck my dick," squealed Robbie. He indulged in a long, satisfying lick of the cone and then opened his mouth, revealing a brown froth swishing around inside.

I think Linda laughed at her brother, and then she tried again to make him go inside, but he wouldn't listen.

His laughter seemed to ricochet off the facade of a nearby tan brick building and then resonate inside my ears. And he kept repeating the little phrase: "Made you look, now suck my dick." He also alternated the wording, saying, "Wanna lick … suck my dick."

I could feel sweat bubbling on my face and neck as an internal rage started to swell and demanded a release. I was standing near Dad's tomato plants. And so after Robbie repeated his mocking phrase, I bent down, scooped up some of Dad's fertilized soil and threw it across the fence at Robbie. The dirt covered almost the entire surface of his ice cream and also smacked him square in the face before settling in his eyes and hair. I rejoiced when his laughter ceased and a frown appeared on his face; he also looked like he was going to start crying. He dropped his dirt-sprinkled cone on the ground and ran away screaming, "I'm gonna tell my mom!"

Linda was still standing near the fence. I shrugged my shoulders and said something like, "sorry, I guess" or, "well, he was asking for it." But she just looked at me with a blank expression and then turned her back and followed her brother across the street to their apartment building.

I must admit I felt proud of my actions. I convinced myself Robbie had provoked me to a point where a response was needed.

I awaited repercussions from Mrs. Blackwood. I was nervous all through dinner that night, as I expected her to come marching across the street at any moment, bang on our screen door and start swearing at me and demanding repayment for the ice cream cone.

But it never happened; no retaliation came.

I thought I got away with it. Or did I?

I think I may have told my parents about the incident later that night, just before bed, when the guilt had started weaving its way through me. I don't remember what they said, but most likely they told me to go to bed and apologize to Robbie the following day. They may have also suggested I give him some money to make up for the ice cream.

But I don't think they meted out any punishment. And as for Linda, Robbie, and me, we remained friends and continued to play together the rest of that summer.

The ice cream event did not ruin their lives. They forgot about it in a couple of days. I think that's because childhood is all about living in the present. You're not thinking about yesterday because you're always looking forward to what's next; you're always searching for the next fun thing to do.

So then why does it stay with me? Why does this scene still haunt me? Maybe it's because the image of the dirt covering the cone remains so vivid in my mind. I can close my eyes and feel the hot sun on my neck. I can see a rivulet of chocolate ice cream sliding down Robbie's forearm. I can picture the hurt and disappointment on his face when the dirt hit the cone and he realized it was ruined, that he wouldn't be able to take another lick. I can see the cone lying on the ground at the base of the fence. I can see Robbie's squat body running away.

But there's something else. I think the reason I threw the dirt on the cone was because I thought I was better than the Blackwoods. I was getting angry as Robbie was teasing me, and in that moment— right before I reached down to grab the dirt—I thought of him like other people did, as nothing but a "wellie," just white trash. And I was also jealous. They had something I didn't, and some sickness in me wanted to take it away. I thought, "If I can't have ice cream, then you shouldn't either."

My family wasn't rich, but we could have had ice cream just about anytime we wanted. All my sister and I had to do was ask our mother or father to buy some at the store. The Blackwoods were different. How much did it set Mrs. Blackwood back to give Linda and Robbie some change for the ice cream man? Where else would she have to save to make up for it? This was a special treat for them, and I wrecked it.

Of course, I was only about nine-years-old at the time. I was irrational and immature—a stupid, selfish kid. But if I start to think about the incident and relive the memory again, I feel ashamed when I see myself stealing Robbie's joy.

I think we moved away from the neighborhood around 1978 or '79, and I never saw Robbie or Linda again. Our house at 126 Stanwix Street is no longer standing. It was demolished by the city several years ago.

In 2011, when I was visiting my mother and stepfather at their home in Rome, I went for a long walk on a clear summer evening. I walked southbound on James Street, heading toward Gansevoort Park and St. Peter's Church. When I got near the police station and the court house, I crossed the street and started walking on Stanwix Street.

As I scanned the block, I realized not much had changed in the neighborhood. It still looked ragged. Some of the small front lawns needed mowing, a tan cat was crossing the street, and a kid's bike was lying on its side in a driveway. And if you can believe this, a white Mr. Ding-A-Ling truck was parked at the curb, and the man inside was selling ice cream treats to customers.

I thought about Linda and Robbie; I wondered where they were and what they had done with their lives. Were they still in Rome? Were they both married? Did they have kids of their own? Was their mother still around? And what happened with their father?

Of course, I had no way of finding out the answers to the questions that came flooding to me as I stood on Stanwix Street.

I wished Linda and Robbie would have appeared on the block at that moment, walking westbound on Stanwix Street toward James Street. I wanted to see them again and offer to buy them both ice cream cones to make up for what I had done and what was lost as a result.

Paul Buchanan

Contemplating Suicides

1974

I'll start with Brendan, a fellow misfit in junior high. In the two years I knew him, Brendan spoke constantly about killing himself. As we walked home from school, his manic monologue might pinball from algebra to suicide to M*A*S*H, without any sense of disproportion. One afternoon, when the two of us were alone in his house, he pulled open a dresser drawer and showed me the neatly folded Beatles t-shirt he was saving to wear when he killed himself.

Both Brendan and I aspired to be fiction writers. I had never actually filled an entire page with prose, but Brendan had typed a 28-page sci-fi novella that owed a heavy debt to *Star Trek*. He let me read it a few weeks before he died. I don't remember it well, and I don't know if it was any good, but there must have been something to recommend it, given that I read it start to finish.

Brendan lugged a hibachi in from the back patio one Wednesday after school. He stuffed clothes into the crack under his bedroom door and lit the charcoal. He was fourteen.

I don't know who found him. I don't know if he was wearing his Beatles shirt. If there was a memorial, none of us from school were invited.

The yearbook from the previous year featured large black-bordered photos of two schoolmates who had died (one in a firearms accident, one killed by his step-father). Brendan didn't get a memorial page. He died in October, so perhaps school photos hadn't been taken yet. Or, perhaps, like burial on sacred ground, the stigma of suicide ruled that honor out.

The idea that suicide is a sin was introduced to western culture fifteen centuries ago. "No suicide described in the Bible is spoken of in terms of condemnation," David J. Mayo writes in *Journal of Personal & Interpersonal Loss:*

> and the historian Gibbon (1947) notes that some early sects of Christians, convinced that martyrs would be gathered under the throne of God, sought martyrdom by taunting Romans until they were

executed. This disturbed St. Augustine, who responded in the 5th century with Biblical and other religious arguments to the effect that suicide was contrary to God's will. Augustine's condemnation of suicide became church doctrine at the Councils of Orleans, Braga, and Toledo in the 6th century and eventually found its way into law throughout Europe and the United States. As recently as a century ago, attempting suicide was not only illegal in Great Britain but was a capital offense.

1981

Wyatt served with the Navy in Nam and was aboard the USS Kitty Hawk during its famous race riot of 1972. When his tour was up, he enrolled in college on the GI Bill and majored in business.

Wyatt was a decade older than the rest of us in the dorm, and he never seemed at ease in our company. He lived on the floor above mine. I remember him as slight and stooped, a milquetoast-type with wire-rimmed glasses and a nasal voice you might not detect a few yards away. He shuffled around campus with hands dug deep in his pockets and had trouble holding eye contact. Our junior year he had a crush on the girl I ended up dating.

Wyatt shot himself through the head several years ago while talking to his wife on the phone. That's all I heard about it.

Real numbers concerning suicide are surprisingly hard to come by. An Australian study of 1,051 "completed" suicides found that only about a third left notes, which means that many deaths must remain ambiguous. Was her Seconal overdose intentional? Did he fall from the balcony or did he jump?

And even if we can clearly establish direct intent in a death, what qualifies as a true suicide? Edwin Shneidman, the father of modern suicidology, wrote this in a piece for *American Scholar:*

> I learned from a study I once did with the coroner of Marin County, California, that more than a quarter of all deaths—all deaths, not just overt suicides—are probably interlaced with threads of imprudence, disregard, excess, indifference, or ennui that bring an end to life sooner than is necessary. In other words, some people who have died what I call "subintentioned deaths" from heart attacks or automobile accidents may have a good deal in common with people who are termed "suicides." In that sense alone, suicide is everybody's business, and we disregard it at the risk of moving up the dates on our own tombstones.

Taking into account the complexities of defining, let alone quantifying, suicide, the U.S. Center for Disease Control offers some estimates:

- In 2007 there were more than 34,000 suicides in the U.S., the equivalent of 94 suicides per day.
- Males took their own lives at nearly four times the rate of females and represented 79% of all U.S. suicides.
- Suicide was the seventh leading cause of death for males and the sixteenth for females.
- Suicide rates for males were highest among those aged 75 and older.
- Suicide rates for females were highest among those aged 45–54.
- Firearms were the most common method of suicide among males (56%).
- Poisoning was the most common method of suicide for females (40.3%).

1985

After college, I worked at a private psychiatric hospital for eight years. On the adolescent unit, where I spent most of my time, I met countless depressed teens who would "perseverate on suicidal themes," as we staff members would write in their medical charts. For many, the talk of suicide seemed an obvious ploy—a way to get attention or to terrorize their parents. (One kid famously rigged a noose to a Genie garage door opener, so his mother would be the one to hang him when she got home from work.)

It wasn't easy to know which kids were being purely manipulative—we took every threat seriously—but there was a flinty lack of flamboyance to some of the kids' threats that could be unnerving.

One such boy, a somber and handsome blond kid who couldn't have been older than sixteen, killed himself after he transferred to another psych hospital. He was on a lockdown unit, on suicide watch, but he managed to swallow a washcloth and choke himself to death.

It's common for reports about suicide, especially the suicide of a young person, to close with a hotline phone number or a campus counseling service to be contacted by readers who might also be contemplating suicide. The assumption seems to be that the tragic death being reported might not have happened if the victim had only sought help from professionals. But the CDC estimates that of the 30,000 U.S. suicides in 2005, about half were under the care of at least one mental health professional at the time of their deaths.

The professionals, themselves, seem to understand their limitations in truly helping the suicidal. A 2011 study of the effects of suicide on the victim's therapist showed that psychologists "typically did not assume responsibility for their client's suicide." As one participating therapist put it, "each of us is responsible for ourselves, and the client did what he had to do."

1990

Jonathan went along on a summer study-abroad trip I led to the UK. A klutzy English major, he dressed expensively and wore a brand of sunglasses so pricy I often found myself teasing him about them. Jonathan told painfully bad jokes and walked with a loose, lumbering gait that had him bringing up the rear on outings.

In our group photos from that trip, Jonathan seems always in the back row, peeking around the others. I only find one photo from those six weeks in which Jonathan isn't partially hidden.

That trip Jonathan spent most of his time with a nursing major I'll call Helen. I assumed it was a budding romance, but Helen, who was the more outgoing and talkative of the two, insisted that Jonathan had a girlfriend back home; their friendship was purely platonic. When we got back to the U.S., Jonathan transferred to a university closer to his Montana family and, presumably, closer to his girlfriend.

A few weeks into the fall semester, Jonathan bought a pistol at a Missoula sporting goods store. He took it back to his dorm room and shot himself through the roof of the mouth.

It was only after his suicide that I learned that Jonathan, who came from a conservative Evangelical family, was gay.

In *The White Album,* Joan Didion talks about our need to fashion our lives into some kind of narrative we can make sense of. The alternative—*senselessness*—is too bleak an option. "We tell ourselves stories in order to live," Didion writes, and later on the same page, "We look for the sermon in suicide, for the social or moral lesson in the murder of five."

So how do we do it? What sermons do we find in the sense-lessness? Valica Boudry, a journalism professor at the University of Wisconsin, compared newspaper coverage of suicides in 1993 and 2003. This was an attempt "to see how suicide was 'framed,' or placed in a social context." In other words, what narrative do we, as a culture, use in talking about suicide? In total, Boudry examined 442 articles and tallied the reasons the reports gave.

Many articles offered no reasons; they just reported a death as a suicide. But, in 1993, eighteen articles mentioned mental illness as the cause, while 140 blamed the suicide on personal problems like custody battles or financial ruin. The articles from 2003 were similarly disproportionate: mental health was mentioned only twenty-eight times, while 107 suicides were attributed to situational problems.

"Americans are in part still blaming individuals for suicide, instead of accepting the role of mental illness…" Boudry concludes. "Culturally, Americans seek to understand why someone would commit suicide instead of accepting mental illness as the likely culprit. The illness is generally the why."

1991

One of the graduate writing programs I attended required us each to take a workshop outside our areas of interest, so that semester Madison and I were the two fiction writers in a class full of poets. I didn't know her very well, but she always chose the seat next to mine, as if, as fiction writers, we needed to stick together.

There was something unkempt and dreamy about Madison—some ineffable quality that made you notice her but want to keep your distance. She spoke in a voice that was mostly sighs, and the things she said were sometimes wince-worthy in their earnest na-ivety, especially amid the brassbound cynicism of a writing program.

In that class we had to workshop a new poem every week, and from the first week we critiqued her work, it was clear the professor had it in for Madison. There were many bad writers in that group, but Madison got singled out each week for a dressing down that made it seem like there was some bad-blood backstory.

About half way through the semester, the professor came back from the break and told Madison she was required in the director's office, down on the third floor, after class.

That night, when we were done, a bunch of us—Madison included—crowded into the elevator. I, who was closest to the door, pressed the buttons for the third floor and the ground floor. The elevator stopped at floor three, and all of us stepped aside so Madison, who was at the back, could get out. She didn't. There was an awkward moment, and then the doors closed, and we all descended in silence those last three floors.

A day or two later, Madison was found hanging in her apartment.

Much of the ethical writing about suicide focuses on end-of-life decisions and medical assistance—the so-called "rational suicides." These are suicides where the people in question are capable of weighing the pros and cons of ending their lives. Words like "terminally ill" and "agony" and "humiliation" appear again and again.

When my father was in hospice care, dying slowly of cancer, the pain tablets we gave him for his breakthrough pain had a warning on the packaging of each dose: Chewing the pills could lead to a rapid and fatal absorption of morphine. The warning struck me as having a kind of subtext: all my father had to do was chew, and his ordeal would be over.

My father didn't chew the pill. His death was slow and brutal. But who could have blamed him if he had? Who would begrudge him that escape from suffering?

2009

Shannon owed me a beer. She was a regular at the bar where I hung out every Thursday night. She was a lean, wickedly funny yoga teacher, who, while sitting on a barstool, could effortlessly tuck both feet behind her head.

Shannon had spent some time in county jail. She never told me why, but she told me all about life in lock-up, in case I ever wanted to use it in a story. She coached me on how to use "sidecar bunkie" in a sentence and how to make mock-enchiladas from the various chips and candies available to prisoners.

The last time I saw Shannon, we didn't get to talk much. She left a few minutes after I sat down next to her. She was in a hurry to leave, holding her credit card aloft and trying to flag down the barkeep. She told me she was heading out to Newport Coast to meet the new man she was seeing. I told her to go ahead and leave; I'd cover her tab. She could buy next week.

A few nights later, Shannon hanged herself from the backyard swing-set at her mother's house. Our mutual friend Adam, another Thursday night regular at the bar, arrived early in the morning to clean the mother's pool. He was the one who found her.

Edwin Shneidman coined the term "psychache" as a way to label a kind of unremitting psychological pain. The agony of "excessively felt shame or guilt, or humiliation, or loneliness, or loss, or sadness, or dread of growing old, or of dying badly."

Schneidman is also the inventor of what's called the "psychological autopsy," an investigation of all the antecedents to a suicide. It's a painstaking reconstruction of what a person did and said and seemed to feel in the days leading up to his or her suicide. It gathers police reports and medical records and the testimony of friends and family.

But Shneidman's two ideas—*psychache* and *psychological autopsy*—seem at odds to me. Can any post-hoc gathering of information ever let us understand the psychache that leads to suicide if we have never felt it ourselves? Can we assume that my father's physical suffering was qualitatively different than the pain that leads a physically healthy woman to hang herself? What could she possibly have said or done or scribbled in a note at her mother's kitchen table that would satisfy our hunger for exegesis?

2010

Tracy was the best writer I knew. She went off to study at an elite New York fiction-writing program. That first year away, she would call me at least once a week in the throes of a panic attack, and I'd have to talk her through the spell until there was some sort of solution or she was just so exhausted from crying she had to sleep.

Two years into her MFA, Tracy lost a lot of weight and started cutting herself with X-Acto blades. By that time, she'd become close friends with one of her professors, who worried about Tracy's wellbeing. The professor got together a small group of colleagues who went by Tracy's apartment one night to talk to her about hospitalization.

Famous writers are sitting on my bed, Tracy texted me. *I think it's an intervention.*

Tracy was hospitalized for two long stretches that spring. While in the psych ward, she wrote all day with pencil and paper. Then, with the one hour she was allowed to use a computer each evening, she would type it up, put it on a thumb drive, and get a visitor to email it to me, so I could call the next day with notes.

Her final unfinished story, which I didn't see until her funeral, was about a girl who got discharged from a mental hospital. The girl bought a man's belt at a department store, and hanged herself on her apartment's fire escape. That's exactly what Tracy did.

The last time I saw Tracy was a few weeks before her death. She and her boyfriend met me at a faux English pub in Glendale. We sat at the bar, with Tracy in the middle. Her boyfriend and I both drank Smithwicks, and Tracy ordered a white Russian. (She was down to 86 pounds, and that was the highest-calorie drink we could think of.)

At one point that afternoon, Tracy rested her left arm on the mahogany bar top, and I could see rows upon rows of precise, deep cuts, like barcodes, on her inner arm.

So, here I have set out to write about a dark, inscrutable human mystery that has crossed my path more often than I can account for. And I have approached it as I approach every other damn thing I write about: I've read books and peer-reviewed monographs, controlled studies and the testimony of experts.

None of it has helped me find what I seem to be looking for.

2012

Jackie downed a bottle of Xanax and called the English department from a convenience store payphone. A colleague and I sped out to her in my Jeep Cherokee, not knowing what we'd find. Jackie was slumped, empty-eyed, on the ground next to the newspaper machines. We packed her into my Jeep, and I steeled myself, trying to think of which ER was closest.

I skidded out of the parking lot in the direction of La Habra Hospital, the place my daughter had been born six years earlier. I ran red lights and careened through corner gas stations. At one point I drove on the wrong side of the road, honking my horn and flashing my high beams.

When I got to the hospital ten minutes later, abuzz with adrenaline, the place had simply vanished. The buildings had been razed, and the empty lot behind the chain link fencing was now a graded field dotted with bulldozers and backhoes.

In a panic, I doubled back in the opposite direction towards Whittier Hospital, which would take us at least another ten or fifteen minutes. I kept looking in my rearview mirror and shouting at Jackie to stay awake.

When we got to the hospital, they rolled Jackie, still breathing, inside on a gurney. They stopped me at the waiting room and told me where I could get some coffee while we waited.

But that was fifteen years ago, and today I'm driving down to San Diego to have a beer with Jackie, now a married thirty-something with two small children.

She said she'd meet me in a pub just off the freeway in Carlsbad, and it turns out to be an old Spires coffee shop that's been transformed into a sports-bar, pool-hall dive. They have Guinness on tap, so I get one and sit at the bar playing Tetris on my iPhone while I wait.

When she arrives, Jackie hugs me like she always does when we meet. She pulls up the barstool next to mine and we talk about our kids and our jobs and all that's happened in the months since the two of us last met. I want to ask her about the Xanax episode since I've been working on this piece, but I'm not sure how to bring it up without making it seem like the sole reason I messaged her last week on Facebook.

But Jackie is fine with talking about it. It's ancient history. So she tells me her side of the story, as she remembers it. It's a story I've never heard until now. The stress of school and family had sent her into a spiral that semester. She'd been seeing a new psychiatrist, who had prescribed a cocktail of psychoactive drugs that made her unsettled and confused.

That afternoon, she swallowed half a bottle of Xanax and then called her psychiatrist. On hearing what Jackie had done, the psychiatrist told Jackie to stay put. She'd call 911, and help would be on its way.

Instead, Jackie grabbed her keys and the pills and ran out to her car.

"I thought the police were after me," Jackie tells me now. She takes a sip from her IPA and sets the glass back on the bar. "She said she was going to call the police, so I took off running."

Jackie had got in her car and started driving. "I was in sweats," Jackie remembers. "And I was trying to get to the beach for some reason, but as I was driving, the road kept going like *this*." She makes a wavy motion with her hand.

Jackie had pulled into the convenience store parking lot and cut the engine because the road was acting so weird, and it didn't feel safe to drive on. "That's when I downed the rest of the bottle," she says.

I try to imagine it—to make sense of it—so I can sort of maybe glimpse the pressure and paranoia building up in her head. But, no, I can't really manage it.

Jackie smiles wryly. "I didn't have the number to the English department," she says, "and I swear I didn't have it memorized, but somehow I dialed it and got Chris. I don't know how I managed it." Chris was the department secretary who came and got me that day.

The rest of the story I know better than Jackie does, and I tell it to her now. But when I'm done with my version, I come up short. I still have no answer. Jackie could have died that afternoon, and that fact still seems unfathomable.

We get a couple more beers and take them into the bar's back room. We throw darts, while a couple of skateboarders play some kind of bean bag toss behind us. Jackie comes from far behind to beat me at cricket, and the whole afternoon turns familiar and warm and comfortable—the way it always does when we get together.

And it occurs to me that this is what Jackie would have been missing if she had died that day: finding a babysitter so she could take an hour or two to play darts with an old friend, before she rushed home to dinner in a house full of books, surrounded by a toy-strewn yard.

When it's time for her to leave, I promise her I won't use her real name in the piece I'm writing. I tell her I haven't used anyone's real name.

Jackie tells me it's okay. I shouldn't worry. She has nothing to be embarrassed about. But a beat later the idea of making up a pseudonym appeals to her. She's always wanted to be called Jackie, though she isn't sure why. I've been taking notes in my Moleskin notebook, and she takes it from me now and jots down all the variants in spelling she can think of—*Jaqi, Jakie, Jacquie*. Watching her grinning and scribbling in my notebook fills me with a deep, wholly senseless wonder. She decides she likes the plain look of *Jackie* best and hands me back my Moleskin.

I settle up our tab and walk her to her car. We hug again—a little longer this time. And I realize how much I needed this—a couple of beers and a game of darts with someone I've known for fifteen years.

In this moment, as I hold her, I feel about as far from death as I've been in a good long time.

Corey Ginsberg

Destination: Alone

"It's just so sad," my mom slurs on the other end of the line, pausing, I assume, to take another sip of vodka. "You're such a nice person, and you're gonna go sit and eat Chinese food alone on the beach."

I stop walking and feel the raindrops latch onto my bare forearms. It hadn't occurred to me that supping on the beach alone in Key West is a sad thing, let alone something so *sad*. I spent most of the day looking forward to this alone time, to getting stoned at the edge of the ocean with a full dinner spread in front of me. It's become an enticing escape plan.

The way my mom says this, though, it's as if I've told her I'll be walking into the Atlantic with my jean pockets stuffed with rocks to wait for the salty tide to envelop me. Nice people should be out with other nice people their age. They should be talking about the Occupy movement, eating pizza and drinking Yuengling. I sip my screwdriver and continue walking.

It's my last night in town for the writers' conference, one I've taken off work to attend and spent hundreds of dollars I can't afford on because Margaret Atwood is teaching. For six days I've been staying at my grandma's house across the island and going to as many of the seminars, meet-and-greets, lectures, and instruction sessions I can stomach. As the days go by my capacity dwindles. I go straight from workshop to the coffee shop to write all afternoon, then pinball around the island for the remainder of the night.

I'm not sure where I'm going. I know where I'm not headed, though—to the open mic event at the Tropic Cinema where most of the writers from my workshop will be reading. The chances of me getting on stage to deliver the first chapter of my novel are as likely as me overcoming my fear of public speaking, as well as my increasing dread of being in public, in the next twenty minutes. The realization upon viewing photos of how miserable I look in workshop interacting with others put a cap on my decision to spend my last night alone.

In the pictures taken during Atwood's workshop throughout the week, my shoulders are squared off in a position that shields me, turtle shell, from the rest of the world. Every camera angle reveals a person who is desperate to look busy but at the same time transparently self-conscious. I'm puffy from lack of sleep and over-indulgence, from a week of too much scotch and not enough goat cheese tart. I look sad, apart, dangling. This host of insecurities I'd always thought lived invisibly inside of me had spilled out; photo after photo is proof.

For so many reasons it's undesirable to be thirty and on the phone with your mother, vying for the title of the drunkest, a position I realize an hour into the conversation she has won, hands-down. My dad is out of town for a deposition, which means my brother, sister and I are on standby, prepared with an arsenal of *um-hmmms*. I apportion these as I walk past the stretch of drag clubs, art galleries and coffee shops, the storefronts partially shielding me from the wind and cool January drizzle.

As much as I'd like to claim to feel burdened by my mom's call, it's good to be on the phone with someone. Being the person engaged, the one who has someone on the other end of the line—it's a largely unobtrusive break from the monotony of my monologue. And it makes my isolation less apparent.

"Wow, look at *her*," some of the onlookers may be thinking. "The blonde in the Teenage Mutant Ninja Turtle T-shirt and unwashed jeans, she's talking on a cellular telephone. I'll bet she has a vibrant social life. Someone must really love her. She won't be alone for long."

Alone. How complicated alone is. Alone is okay if you're seques-tered. In a crowd, though, being on the outskirts is obvious and awkward. At a conference like this, among writers with whom I at least share some unspoken bond invisibly woven by the toil of the craft, I feel more alone than I do almost anywhere else. Standing like a maimed lion apart from the pack at cocktail parties, too nervous to eat, too awkward to walk up to a stranger and start a conver-sation, drinking too quickly, excessively fidgeting with bev naps and plastic cutlery, wondering why I kidded myself into thinking I could mingle this time—it never seems to get better. The night eventually collapses into me taking off, walking to Subway, getting a footlong veggie sub and eating it on the pier while I write a poem on stray sheets of paper. Even in Atwood's workshop I sit at the end of the table, quietly jotting notes and hoping none of the other eleven participants notice, let alone comment, on my awkwardness. This morning, though, the woman sitting next to me turned from the round-table discussion and said, "You're so quiet. Are you getting anything out of this?"

As my mom's rambling about her new diet, about how delicious plain Boca Burgers are after eating nothing but powdered eggs, soy bars and pickles for two days, I keep walking. In the nearly two hours I've been on the phone with her I've been up and down Duval Street twice and veered onto many of the side roads, ravenously looking in windows, getting progressively wetter. I've seen nearly every overpriced hookah, offensive T-shirt and slutty dress/hoop-earring combo the island boasts. The smells of falafel, pizza and hot dogs waft from restaurants and street vendors.

With each step my feet scream to please stop walking, to sit still—just for ten minutes. Someplace out of the wind and rain. I want so much to go into a bar, to pull up a chair next to a group of people and nurse a Cosmo or Corona like a normal human. I want to have someone turn to me and say, "How 'bout the weather?" while I eat french fries and stare at the few stragglers traveling solo. But the more I window shop for a place that I could let myself go into, the less likely it becomes that I'll stop. My mantra has already become motion, my beat measured by the compulsory clomping of my heels.

Toward the end of Duval Street is a stretch of drag clubs. Since it's nearing show time, I know many of the performers will be standing outside, trying to lasso passersby with their compliments and blown kisses. "Hon-ney, love those ear-rings," one of the queens shouted at me last night as I walked to the pier with my sub, bag of Chex Mix, and Strongbow. What if one of them points out how many times I've shuffled past? I turn down a quiet side road and keep walking, completing a square of turns until I'm back on the main street.

As the algae bloom of alcohol and pot flowers in my brain, I pass Spider-Man, who's sitting Indian-style on the sidewalk, strumming a sitar. In Key West this isn't supposed to be strange. He's as much a staple as the roosters roaming the streets. This is the fifth or sixth time I've walked past him today. He looks up, as he always does, his metallic mask eyes catching the light of the liquor store sign he's positioned in front of. Usually not one to engage tourists, Spider-Man signals to me—a simple, lone nod—as if to say, *You again. Back already?* I feel my cheeks redden as I pretend not to notice him noticing me. At least he doesn't speak; having my social anxiety pointed out by a Marvel character as he plays a Ravi Shankar song would be too much tonight.

As my mom begins to tell me, again, about waterproofing the basement, my mind flashes back to traveling to Greece last spring, to eating alone in my hotel room at night, taking in mouthfuls of bread and feta, drinking liters of two-Euro wine and looking out the windows at the setting sun over the Aegean Sea. All the restaurants on Paros I'd walked past earlier that afternoon were quaint, authentic, perfect. I would have had a fantastic meal in any of them. I couldn't risk it, though. Going in, sitting alone, knowing how likely it was that nobody would talk to me—it'd be like the cafeteria in seventh grade all over again. My awkwardness followed me six thousand miles to Europe. Maybe it will follow me anywhere.

Both times I've trekked the main street I've ended up back at this derelict Chinese restaurant, its neon sign beckoning me from the parking lot: *Hey, I'm deserted. You can come inside and nobody will notice. Place a to-go order, then take it away and eat it alone.* Destiny has teamed up with a subconscious, marijuana-driven craving for something salty and fried to bring me here.

"I'm gonna get some dinner," I say to my mom. I've been trying to get her to wind up the discussion for ten minutes.

She seems genuinely shocked. "You're not really going in by yourself?" My mom knows I've inherited her phobia of solitary public dining, and that like her, I'd rather skip dinner than sit alone in public eating it.

"I love you," I say. "Drink some water." I hang up before she can object.

Fifteen minutes later, with my bag of food in hand, I walk toward Higgs Beach on the end of the island closer to where my grandma lives. Despite having no sense of direction, I'm generally able to retrace my steps by noticing landmarks and unique shrubs from earlier. I've spent years perfecting this strategy, which generally works if I pay close enough attention to where I've been. The only problem is this time I was on the phone and didn't do enough noticing. Now it's dark and the rain is picking up, and I can't remember if I should make a left at the white house with the hammock, or turn right onto the street with the lit-up Christmas tree in the front yard.

Earlier in the day my grandma pointed out how likely it was I'd get lost, and how shocking it was I hadn't already. This is the first trip to the Keys she hasn't forced me to take the inevitable folded map of the island, a relic I insist, time after time, I have no use for as my brain can't spatially process maps. There's no way I'm going to call her for directions only to hear the familiar grunt and *told-you-so,* envisioning her tanned face tighten into a smirk. I will figure this out on my own.

I'm on an island; how hard can it be to find the ocean? I had opted for these damned heels instead of my standard tennis shoes, hoping that would make me more likely to go into a restaurant, to be around others. *How stupid,* says the stress fracture in my ankle. I should have known my capacity better. The wind makes it hard to walk, but I push on, clutching the bag of food, trying to spot familiar structures.

Being lost and alone is a compounding endeavor, one that starts with an initial wrong turn and snowballs into another and another, culminating, as I learned on a previous visit to Key West, into losing all sense of internal calibration and ending up at the Naval Air Station at four a.m. It's a claustrophobic sensation because there's no promise of an escape route. Being lost can, and often does, get much worse before it's solved. Which is why, thirty minutes later, I end up on the other side of the island at what appears to be a locked-up cemetery. It must be the one I've heard mentioned at least a dozen times by conference attendees, the one I've tried to find myself during the daytime. The white bars of the gate announce its inaccessibility.

I peer in and feel a sense of comfort that corresponds with looking at the dead. It feels right to be here now. Only by this point I'm the kind of hungry-shaky that demands immediate attention and can't wait another city block for sustenance. It may be midnight by the time I find the ocean. Having nothing in my stomach since the caramel frappe at lunch has taken its toll.

All night I'd been trying to hold back until I got to my destination—my swatch of seclusion—to eat. A graveyard, it seems, is the next closest thing to being completely alone. I can't possibly look that bad or awkward among corpses, and the dead won't comment on my action plan for the evening. I slouch onto the cement wall by the front gate and fish my hand into the bag for one of the egg rolls.

As I stare at the largest of the tombstones by the road I imagine the other writers at the last night festivities, reading their chiseled words to one another, pausing for the inevitable bout of applause, then heading down the road for conch fritters and drinks with bamboo umbrellas. An oily runoff drips down my chin and collects below the collar of my shirt as I scarf down the first half of an overcooked egg roll. I lean against the cool metal bars for support.

Just as I let myself exhale, a man and a woman walk down the street holding hands. They look into the cemetery, then at me eating, then back at the rows of tombstones. I wonder if I'm being disrespectful. Tacky, maybe. And desperate, yes. If nothing else it's creepy. *So sad.* I shove the half-eaten nub into my mouth, zip my hooded sweatshirt to cover the mess, and begin walking again.

Enough wrong turns eventually yield a convoluted path toward a destination.

It takes nearly forty more minutes to find Higgs Beach. During the final hundred or so yards I take to walking with my legs shoulder-width apart, a duck-like diaper plod, which I've found alleviates some of the stress on my ankle. I waddle past the AIDS memorial, veer off the concrete, and slink directly onto the beach, my heels marshmallowing into the sand. The only people around me are two homeless men on a park bench wrapped in camouflaged sleeping bags, and some hippies playing bongo drums on the pier.

The sand is damp and chilly, a cool anchor to my sweaty legs. I don't have a blanket, so I flop onto the beach and let the denim absorb the ocean's backwash. I open the plastic container of eggplant with garlic sauce and the tightly packed box of white rice. This meal is the main attraction, the *pièce de résistance,* my justification for the night's meandering. The remaining egg roll slides out of the bag like a slug, the tail of grease leaving a reverse map on the bag.

There's so much food, and the prospect of this meal makes me smile wider than anything has all day. Even sitting next to Margaret Atwood. Even watching the sun retract into a purple tongue over the island. Even finishing the essay I've been torturing myself with for months. Now I feel the appropriateness of where I am: sitting on the beach in a windstorm, watching the waves topple, absorbing the sideways spray on my face from thirty feet back. Alone, finally. Apart and alone. I reach down for the chopsticks.

But where are they? I peek into the empty bag and run my hand over the sand. There has to at least be the standard-issued spork/tissue-thin folded napkin combo. There's soy sauce and that funny orange gel, but that's it.

I have options. I could go to a convenience store on Duval Street and ask for a plastic fork and a napkin. But the prospect of walking another mile in these boots that were clearly not made for walking is unfathomable. I could save the food for later and head back to my grandma's house, where it's warm and dry, and there are plenty of eating utensils and places to sit. But she'll still be awake and will remark not only about the quantity of food ordered *(Who's going to eat all of that?),* but also note that I should be out with the other writers during my last night in town *(Why come to a conference and not go to anything?).* The best option, I realize, is to stay right where I am. And dig in.

I want this meal to be delicious, transcendent. The most perfect eggplant birthed by the vegetable kingdom, fried into spongy submission and tossed with those savory chemicals they throw in when nobody's looking. I want this meal to be my hindsight beacon; when I'm miles away in the morning, watching the island shrink in my rearview mirror as I boomerang back to Miami, rehearsing my litany of regrets and should-have-dones in my loose-fitting gym shorts while I plan my cranberry juice cleanse, I want this meal to have been so, so worth it. Because if it's not, where does that leave me?

I dump the soy sauce and orange goop on the mound of dinner, stir it with my index finger, and use the remaining egg roll as a fork-shovel. Even by my low standards and unrefined, not-so-far-removed-from-grad-school palate, this is the most mediocre, over-fried, C-minus Chinese food I've ever had. The garlic sauce tastes like Crisco and corn starch, and the egg rolls are the consistency of gym socks stuffed with chewed cabbage. I could stop eating. But I don't. I should be at the open mic night. But I'm here instead. I ought to be comfortable around ten other writers, ten other anybodys. But I'm not.

There's a gritty consistency to the food, which at first I assume is an uneven pocket of MSG. After swallowing enough, though, I realize my dinner Combination Plate H7 is granular and abrasive, and what I'm eating is mouthfuls of sand, which have latched onto the lumps of eggplant. I do my best to brush off the topmost layer, but it's combined with the surface oil to form congealed brown gravy. It's well past that point in the meal when I should concede, when I should go back to my grandma's house, pour a nightcap, and finish my poem. But I haven't come this far to placate myself into a half-binge. I shove my right hand in, ball up some rice, and keep eating.

My mom's words resonate, a goddamn reel that won't mute itself: *so sad.* I imagine her driving to the beach and shaking her head, just like she used to when she'd pick me up after basketball practice in middle school and see me sitting on a bench apart from the rest of the team. I imagine her rolling down her window and watching her thirty-year-old daughter suck down food like a starved POW as wind sandblasts her. The mom in my imagination sighs her token sigh and shakes her head the way only my mom can. She rolls up the car window and drives away.

By the time the last morsels of rice have been plucked by index finger and thumb, and the remaining river of garlic oil has been poured into a corner of the Tupperware trough then siphoned down my gullet, I'm awkwardly, though not unbearably, full. I've used nearly an entire tablet's worth of paper to blot oil from my hands and face. Sand has blown onto my cheeks and left me with a slick ocean beard. Even in the dark I can tell that I'm a mess.

It's officially the end of the meal, which means it's also the end of the vacation. I slowly brush the sand from my jeans, take off my shoes and socks, and begin the mile trek to my grandma's house. How heavy I am.

Although it feels like it's got to be after midnight, my cell phone says it's not yet ten. If I go back, my grandma will still be awake, will ask questions. She'll no doubt wonder why I smell like China Town and sweat, why I'm barefoot and limping. She'll say, *You were lost, weren't you? I knew you should've taken the map.* She'll want to hear how the reading went, what I had for dinner. Over the course of the night I've grown accustomed to the sound of my thoughts, which by now feel more like a cul-de-sac than a one-way street. I can't morph them into a two-lane highway yet.

The last meal doesn't have to stop here. There's still time for ice cream, and if I push hard enough I know I can fit it in. The idea hits me with such a force I nearly trip on an uneven sidewalk slab. Conveniently, there's a Dairy Queen two blocks from my grandma's house, and I know from passing it on my morning run that it's open till ten tonight. Returning to that spot will mean I've journeyed full circle. According to the clock on my phone I've got eight minutes to make it a half mile, which is doable if I book it. I put my balled-up socks and boots back on and set off in a trot.

The woman at Dairy Queen doesn't see me wobbling down the road. If she understood my newly acquired urgency, she'd know better than to flip that neon orange sign to CLOSED at 9:58, right as I approach the parking lot.

I slow my pace, though I keep walking. Each step feels pre-programmed, inevitable, as I head across the street and around the block. My body knows that I've already committed to riding this binge as far as I can.

Ten minutes later I sit on the root of a banyan tree and dump out my bag of loot. I'm a block from my grandma's house, and I hope she doesn't happen to be out walking her pug. How would I explain myself? Onto the dry, cool dirt I pour my bounty: a pint of Ben and Jerry's Chocolate Fudge Brownie ice cream, a pack of Soft Batch chocolate chip cookies, and a fork and napkin I made sure to request from the attendant at the Chevron station on the corner.

So sad. My mom won't remember saying this to me. Tomorrow the pieces of our conversation will blur in her mind the way dreams swim together upon waking. But I'll remember.

A few late-night walkers pass me as I crumble soft cookies into the quickly melting brown slop. I wonder if it's weird to be eating dessert on the wet ground in some stranger's yard at ten thirty on a Wednesday. Then I remember I'm in Key West, and nothing is that weird.

A man walking a poodle lets his eyes linger on me as I lift huge, dripping forkfuls to my mouth. Then he moves on. He must think I'm a benign homeless person or one of the island's crazy cat ladies. Maybe I look happy sitting here. Not awkward, not ashamed. By this point I'm too tired for any of that. Maybe if someone were to take my photograph as I scrape out that last cold glob, my perpetual frown would be curled at the edges into a sad sort of smile.

Lockie Hunter

Remembering Vera

Before it gained momentum, swelling every hour, before the swamp water lapping against boats and the wind scratching the Spanish moss were met with something new: a larger, warmer water, a larger, warmer wind. Before the extreme rage of the storm was met with disbelief. Before the water pounded against the levee, mincing it, allowing the swirling ocean to hurtle down the historic streets, flashing into the schools, ripping up telephone poles, and gutting the first floor of every home, betraying promises of safety. Before the wind tossed a thirty-foot sailboat onto the roof of a church, the boat's mast a new, grotesque steeple. Before one man jumped from the upper level seats of the Superdome to his death rather than face another hour. Before there was no land-line phone service or radio. Before there was no water, no insulin, no baby formula, no gasoline, no band-aids.

Before the levee broke and water separated children from the parents. Before it forced an eleven year old girl into the "safety" of the Superdome only to be subjected to the threat of rape. Before a French Quarter couple shot one another screaming *we are going to die anyway.* Before the security guard's mother was trapped in the St. Bernard nursing home. Before she heard her son say, *Yeah, Momma, somebody's coming to get you. Somebody's coming to get you on Tuesday. Somebody's coming to get you on Wednesday. Somebody's coming to get you Thursday. Somebody's coming to get you on Friday*—before the mother drowned Friday night alone. Before the people of New Orleans began to realize that help was not coming, that they were trapped, condemned. Before its impact was grossly underestimated. Before flood waters sent the newlyweds into their Bourbon Street attic with little breathing room left. There was a Monday morning in a city where the graves of the dead never lacked flowers. A place where petite wild parrots flickered in the oak trees on restaurant terraces, where fresh sugar cane was still sold by the stick in open-air markets. Nine a.m., an hour when you would be taking beignets under lazy rotating fans. New Orleans, birthplace of Louis Armstrong, *A Streetcar Named Desire,* Truman Capote, Lagniappe, and a pink libation called the Hurricane. And for a few remaining moments, the Spanish moss, having draped for generations, still hung on the cypress. The musicians vacated Preservation Hall. The trombone was packed tightly in a waterproof case. A grandmother in a wheel-chair kissed her grandchild on the forehead, watched her son-in-law latch their Garden District plantation shutters, waited and prayed.

Afterward the nation heard *Heck of a job, Brownie.* Afterward we lost part of our history. A corpse of an elderly man lay wrapped in a child's bed sheet decorated with Batman, one shoe on, one shoe off in a cart on Rampart Street. A power line lay in the street next to a child's jump rope. Afterward the grandmother in the wheel chair died of fluid in her lungs. *We can't just leave her here alone,* the child pleaded. *We have no choice,* the mother said. The child kissed her grandmother's forehead and hugged her, and the mother placed a bag over her head and left her on the sidewalk of New Orleans. Afterward, there were corpses in the water. If there was rope, they were tied down so they wouldn't float away. Often there was no rope.

On September 4th, just days after the impact, a few dozen people gathered for the annual New Orleans decadence parade. A street musician wearing a sombrero and a guitar slung over his back, said, *It's New Orleans, man.* We're going to celebrate. A day in a town that likes to rejoice. The camera panned out to the Garden District, a woman's body lay at the corner of Jackson Avenue and Magazine Street: a short wall of bricks was built around the body, holding down a plastic tarpaulin. On it, someone had spray-painted a cross and the words, *Here lies Vera. God help us.* The graves of the dead no longer had flowers.

Melissa Grunow

Threat

> *A fire burns along the eastern rim*
> *of mountains. In the valley we*
> *see it as a celestial prank, for*
> *in the summer haze the mountains*
> *themselves are lost, but as the night*
> *deepens the fire grows more golden*
> *and dense.*
> *—Philip Levine, "Fire"*

It's like hearing the *pop* when bat connects with ball, but the ball pivots and spins and flies away from the outfield, into the stands, and straight at my head. However, instead of sitting in the lower deck on a sunny day, I am seated in the driver's seat negotiating with fresh snow as it falls to the ground and freezes, and instead of a ball heading toward me, it's an oncoming car that spins around and slides toward my vehicle sideways, lining up like clapping hands to smash in my driver's side door.

For a moment, I see the outcome of the impact, hear the crunch of car on car, and feel my body shoved up onto the center console as my side of the car accordions into itself. I hear glass break, see nothing but my hands shielding my face, and feel my body stiffen then collapse. I'm zapped with cold air and attacked by snow coming in through the broken window. Shards of glass slip out of my hair, and my legs twist and get stuck under the steering wheel.

But the thought only lasts a moment. Instead, I jerk the steering wheel to the right and my engine revs in defense as the wheels pull themselves up onto the curb. The car rolls along the grass, turns onto concrete, and comes to a stop at the exit of a parking lot.

"Whoa, nice driving," Leslie says as I hear her exhale.

I put the car in park and open the door; I climb out and look around, expecting to see destruction in my wake. Leslie walks the perimeter of the car to check for damage: a cracked bumper, broken axle, popped tire. But there's nothing, not even a scratched hubcap from going up the curb.

Thirty feet away, the other car is stopped at an angle, straddling the two lanes. The driver runs to me screaming, "Are you OK?!" then throws his arms around my neck and hugs me for longer than

I've hugged my mom, let alone a stranger.

"I thought I was going to die!" he says. "I thought you were going to die! Oh my god, I think I'm in shock!" I hug him back, trying to calm him down, and also trying incredibly hard to not laugh. I'm not mad. I'm not panicked. More than anything, I'm bewildered, still not entirely certain about what just happened. I just know that the threat is over; everyone is safe.

"Are you OK to drive?" I ask him. "Do you want me to call someone for you?"

He points across the street to an apartment complex about half a block away. "I was almost home."

"You should probably move your car. It's OK. Everything is OK."

He apologizes again and runs back to his car. Before he gets in he turns back and yells, "I promise I'll drive slower."

Dusk settles on the horizon, casting darkness across the grass. I stack wood inside the outdoor chimney and click the lighter multiple times before it lights. As the flames grow, I sit back in my chair and watch it intently, hear the crackling, and feel a light breeze move through the yard. It's the first fire of spring, warming the cool nights on the patio.

The night is well underway while we lie in bed and watch television, the blankets pulled up around our shoulders, the bedroom dark.

I turn to Jason. "Do hear that?"

He looks at me and shakes his head. "What?"

"That noise."

"It's probably outside." He burrows down under the blankets and gets comfortable. My bedroom window is right above the neighbor's driveway, so it's not an unfair assumption.

"No." I mute the TV. "Listen."

He picks his head up off the pillow and stares at me.

"It sounds like people talking downstairs. Doesn't it?" I shift a little toward the door. A mumbling noise makes its way up through the floorboards, so distinctive that it can't be ignored.

"I'm going to see what it is," I say as I climb out of bed and look around my room, for what I don't know. There's no baseball bat or knife or gun. I'm not that kind of American. I have a rush of courage and head toward the stairs empty-handed.

"Well, I'm coming with you," Jason says, following close behind me, though I'm not sure how much use he'll be. He's two inches shorter and at least forty pounds lighter than I am. Safety in numbers, I guess.

I make my way down the stairs and open the door. I hear voices and realize they're singing voices, with music to back them up.

"It's the Indigo Girls," I say with laughter in my voice. "But where is it coming from?" I turn the corner and walk into the living room to find one of my cats lying on the power button of my docked iPod. The hair on the back of my neck and my arms settles back down onto my skin.

Jason scoffs and stomps back upstairs.

"Phantom," I say to the cat as I shoo him away. "You're really living up to your name."

I turn the power off, close the front room curtains and check the locks on the doors, just in case.

The flames climb over one another, their edges white or green as they spike and then circle across the wood. A log shifts and embers confetti into the air, falling and disappearing like lightning bugs disguised in darkness.

I walk along the Las Vegas strip next to Ian, remembering to keep my bag on the inside of my body, away from the street. We had just stopped at a fountain and could feel the back spray as water connected with water, a mist that cools us just slightly on a warm summer evening.

The street is crowded with people edging past one another. Signs along the way warn against jaywalking, threatening citations from the Las Vegas police.

Up ahead, the crowd shifts in a snake-like motion, the bobbing of heads follow suit as they move around an object on the sidewalk.

Just outside of the Eiffel Tower replica, I see a young police officer with a notepad in his hand talking to small group of people who are seated on the sidewalk, their backs against a concrete wall.

"OK, who saw it?" the officer asks looking from face to face.

"I didn't see it," someone remarks, "but I heard it."

There is a man lying face down on the ground, one arm above his head, the other next to his body, as if he were trying to swim across the sidewalk. He looks crumpled, flattened almost. To my right is a stopped car, a giant hole in the windshield with long cracks inching away from it like the roots of a tree.

Rolling away from the man is a trickle of blood so dark it's almost black. It flows down the sidewalk, pooling next to his knee.

It isn't until I step over his ankle and continue down the street that I realize he is dead.

I open the mesh-covered door and jab at the fire with a poker. The embers pulsate, giving off an underlying glow, a heartbeat.

My neighbor catches my attention one morning before I leave for work. "I wanted to let you know that someone tried to break into our house Sunday night."

I set my coffee mug on top of the car and walk toward him across my front yard. "What happened?"

"My wife had fallen asleep in front of the TV. Around one o'clock in the morning she woke up to someone fiddling with the front door. They were twisting the knob," he reaches his hand out to demonstrate, "but the door was locked. Then she heard them walk around the side, through the gate, and try the side door."

I stand there staring at him. I look to his house and imagine a shadowy figure lurking between our two homes, testing his locks just below my bedroom window.

"We called the police," he says. "But by the time they got here, whoever was trying to get in was long gone."

For weeks, every creak, every squeak, and I'm looking over my shoulder or around a corner, or not, for fear of what I might find. The thump sounds of my cats jumping from the furniture to the floor sounds like footsteps—a person—moving about on the other side of the wall.

I come home from work to find my laptop open. I find the basement door unlatched. I wake up to find I've left the door unlocked all night. Do I invite these opportunities to feel afraid, to create a threat in my own home?

I keep mace in my bedside drawer, mace that was given to me by my parents one Christmas to carry when I went running at night. Now the canister rests in the drawer, the red button just inches from my head each night as I wake to distant sounds of fighting cats, wind against the window, raindrops on the shingles.

I add more kindling to the fire, stacking it carefully, introducing it slowly to the ashy logs. I feel the heat against my skin and my eyes squint at the change in light. Orange flames roll down the side of the new wood, their tips flapping like a flag as they come together and become one.

I'm on break between sessions at a conference, and I watch a woman, a stranger, wearing an oversized hat and dark sunglasses, even though we're indoors and the auditorium lights are dim. I stare because she's so out of place. I think she stares back, but I cannot tell. She produces a half smile and angles her body toward me. An invitation to talk? An opportunity to converse with a fellow writer?

Her get-up reminds me of "Three Girls," a story by Joyce Carol Oates in which two young women recognize Marilyn Monroe in a bookstore, though she is dressed in a disguise. Does this woman have disillusions that she is a celebrity not to be recognized? Why does she hide and in the process of hiding, simultaneously draw attention to herself?

I sit up straight, then look away, take a manuscript out of my bag, and pretend to read. She's odd—too odd for me to tolerate. I already have intense social anxiety when it comes to networking, mingling, or any other word for a situation in which I have to interact with strangers. Interacting with this woman will leave my shoulders tense for days.

Wood crackles then snaps in half, a flame-engulfed log shifts and bumps up against the mesh siding. The cage encloses the fire, but it does not contain it. The paper used as kindling is completely gone, disintegrated, curling into itself as it fades away. But nothing really disappears, nothing is really destroyed; it just changes shape.

It's raining for the third day in a row, and I walk briskly toward my car with my head down. I open the passenger side door and toss in my bags, then walk around the back of the car, keys in hand. There's a van parked next to me, backwards, our driver's doors lined up side-by-side.

A tall, thin man wearing a black sweatshirt with the hood pulled over his head approaches his door at the same time I approach mine. "Oh, excuse me," I say as I turn my back to him, and reach for the handle to climb into my car first.

My head jerks backward, and my keys fall to the ground. The man has me by the back of the hair, his hand tangled in tight.

I twist. He starts to pull, to drag me, and I make myself as heavy as I can while trying to reach behind me to hit, scratch, claw. My fingertips brush against the cool metal of his zipper and drag along the fabric of his sweatshirt. My feet scuttle backward as he pulls me harder, and I can't stand up, I can't fall down.

Don't let them take you. Whatever you do, don't let them take you.

128

The words pop into my head from a news broadcast or a self-defense lecture, I don't know for sure. I listen to the advice and remember the warnings, the statistic of women who are abducted and never return. *Fight like hell,* the voice says. *But don't let them take you.* My shoe grazes over my keys, and I kick them, hard, between my tires so that my car is not an option for him.

It's my last moment of clarity. The pain resonates through my skull to my neck and down my spine. I scream. I feel as though I am minutes, seconds, away from blacking out. I struggle, I grunt, I scream some more.

Through my tears and the rain, against the backdrop of the night sky, I see a clenched fist come toward my face. My eye explodes and explodes again, the fist pulling back and coming toward me over and over.

He doesn't speak. He continues to hit me to shut me up.

Bile collects in my throat and burns. I choke, cough, scream some more. My eyes close, and among the darkness are spots of brightness, like white twinkle lights against a dark house at Christmas. I raise my hands to my head and scratch at his clenched fist that's tangled in my hair, the other draped around my neck and squeezing, but I can't get in there, I can't unwrap the strands from around his fingers. I'm quiet as I struggle to breathe, the heels of my shoes dragging against the asphalt.

The pulling stops. I'm shifted sideways, then dropped to the ground, landing hard, tiny rocks scraping the palm of my hand. I open my eyes, and there is a man bent over me.

"Are you OK?"

I put my hands up and scream some more, inching away from him.

"It's OK! It's OK!" he puts his hands up defensively. "He's gone. Whoever it was, he ran away when he saw me. We've called the police." This man is not wearing a black sweatshirt with a hood. He's not tall or thin. His face is soft and round and caring. His voice is gentle.

I turn and see two women approaching me, one talking into her cell phone, the other staring, horrified.

I bring my hand to my face and lightly stroke my swollen cheek bone. The rain continues to fall, water from the parking lot seeps into my clothes, soaking me.

The man offers me his hand, and I stand up, slowly, my knees untrustworthy. I sway and collapse toward him, and he grabs me, holds me steady, and walks with me to lean me against the bumper of my car. *The bumper.* I was dragged almost ten feet. In how much time? I can't be sure.

For months after I need an escort every time I walk through a parking lot. I don't grocery shop alone or at night. I don't leave my house after dark without a companion.

I still sleep with the light on next to my bed.

Sometimes, the fear is real. Sometimes, the fear is valid.

The flames are quiet, the logs white with ash. The sky has darkened. I move the embers around with the poker to cool them, the first bonfire of summer coming to an end. In the distance I hear the whirring of cars on the freeway and the night air drop a cool breeze onto my shoulders. I pour water over the remains and hear the sizzle, the sound fire makes when it's dying. The soot mixes with the water and leaves a thick paste where there once was heat.

I'm walking along the mountain foothills in the desert, wishing I'd had enough sense to change out of my flip-flops and into closed-toe shoes. There are seven of us, and all the people around me are strangers, people I didn't know twenty-four hours ago, whose last names I'm still learning.

We stay on a path the width of a one-lane dirt road. Tumble weeds and prickly pear cacti stand quietly around us, deeply rooted in the ground or the side of the hill. If we listen, we can hear the movement of the Rio Grande that flows just on the other side of the brush.

I look over my shoulder at the distance we've covered. I feel like we've gone too far, but I don't speak up. The sun is moving further and further west and we continue to walk. We step over a cable suspended between two poles bearing a sign that reads, "Private Property. No Trespassing," and keep walking.

We gather in the ruins of an abandoned silo, where nothing remains save for a short concrete wall—decorated with graffiti—and piles of rocks, broken cinder blocks, and old metal grates. When I stand near a metal structure in the center, my voice bounces throughout the remains of the building, echoing in stereo. There are remnants of memories here, but they keep their secrets. We'll never know what this building was for or why or when it was destroyed.

It's nearly dark. We turn to head back, and I stay centered on the road, for fear of rattlesnakes or other wildlife defending their territory. We come around a bend and head back to toward the neighborhood. It's so dark I find myself squinting to see the ground in front of me, and I have to force myself to relax my eyes.

Up ahead we can see the outline of a person walking toward us. I feel my body stiffen and fall one step behind Jada and Blake. We get closer and it's an old woman out for an evening stroll, as it's much cooler once the sun goes down.

"It's so nice to see other people out here," she says as she passes us.

I relax my body as Blake's feet scuffle against the gravel. "Does that freak you out to see someone walking toward you in the dark, or is it just me?"

Jada chuckles and makes a reassuring joke that the old woman is probably non-threatening, and I mutter in agreement. I don't speak of the impending fear I feel with each new experience, with every unfamiliar interaction. Instead, I quicken my step to fall in line with them again and keep walking.

ABOUT THE CONTRIBUTORS

Brian Forrest
Spies: Elizabeth Thorpe / Codename: Cynthia
Ink on paper
12" x 9"

POETRY

Jennifer L. Collins is a tattooed poet and animal lover who has been reluctantly transplanted from the south, and now lives with her husband and creatures in Pittsburgh, PA. Her poetry has been published in various journals, including Chelsea, The Potomac Review, and *Redivider,* and nominated for a Pushcart by *Puerto Del Sol.* She currently works as the Assistant Director of a Writing Center, and spends her summers as an instructor of creative writing and drama at the Cardigan Mountain School in Canaan, NH.

Brad Garber lives and writes in Lake Oswego, Oregon. He has published poetry in *Cream City Review, Alchemy, Fireweed, Uphook Press, Front Range Review, TheNewerYork, Ray's Road Review, Flowers & Vortexes, Emerge Literary Journal, Generation Press, Penduline Press, Dead Flowers, New Verse News* and other quality publications. Nominee: 2013 Pushcart Prize for his poem, "Where We May Be Found."

Christina Matekel-Gibson recieved a BA in English from Brigham Young University in Idaho. She was born and raised in San Francisco, but currently lives in Oklahoma, where she teaches preschool. She has been published in *Penny Ante Feud, Sphere, Poetry Superhighway, Portmanteau,* and *Broad*.

Ryan Havely earned his MFA in Fiction from Minnesota State and his BA in English and Creative Writing from Ohio University. He teaches various forms of writing at West Virginia University at Parkersburg. His work has been published in such literary magazines, such as *Midwestern Gothic, Mobius, Dappled Things,* and *The Columbia Review.*

Michael Hemmingson lives in Baja and southern California. His collection of stories, *Pictures of Houses with Water Damage,* is available from Dzanc Books. His poetry has appeared in *Hobart, South Dakota Review, Hiram Poetry Review, The New Republic,* and elsewhere.

Sarah Katharina Kayß *1985 in Koblenz (Germany), studied Comparative Religion and Modern History in Germany and Britain. In autumn 2012, she became a PhD candidate at the War Studies Department of King's College London. Her artwork, essays and poetry have appeared in literary magazines, journals and anthologies in Germany, Switzerland, Austria, the United Kingdom, Italy, Canada, New Zealand and the United States. Sarah is a recipient of the Austrian-VKSÖ Prize (2012) and winner of the manuscript-award of the German Writers Association (2013). In autumn 2013 her poetry and prose collection "I like the world the way it is" (editions trèvès) will be published in Germany. She edits the bilingual literature magazine *The Transnational* (former: *PostPoetry*) and lives in London.

Cindy E. King, originally from Cleveland, Ohio, currently lives in Lancaster, Texas, where she teaches at the University of North Texas Dallas as an Assistant Professor of English and Writing. Her most recent publications include poems in Callaloo, The North American Review, the African American Review, the American Literary Review, Jubilat, and *Barrow Street.* Her work can also be heard online on *American Weekend,* a production of National Public Radio, at http://weekendamerica.publicradio.org/display/web/2008/12/13/cocktail_hour, at http://rhinopoetry.org (RHINO Poetry), and at http://www.pankmagazine.com/category/2011/8-5-may-2013/ (PANK Magazine).

John McKernan, who grew up in Omaha Nebraska, is now a retired comma herder / Phonics Coach after teaching 41 years at Marshall University. He lives mostly in West Virginia, where he edits *ABZ Press.* His most recent book is a selection of poems *Resurrection of the Dust.* He has published poems in *The Atlantic Monthly, The Paris Review, The New Yorker, Virginia Quarterly Review, The Journal, Antioch Review, Guernica, Solstice* and many other magazines.

Ralph Monday is an Associate professor of English at Roane State Community College in Harriman, TN. His work has appeared in publications such as *The Phoenix, Bitter Creek Review, Impressions, Kookamonga Square, Deep Waters, Jacket Magazine,* and *PoetryRepairs.* He is the featured poet in PoetryRepairs for the December 2013 issue. He also paints and has an exhibit currently on display.

Brianna Pike currently lives in Indianapolis where she is an Associate Professor of English at Ivy Tech Community College. She teaches creative writing, literature and composition courses and earned her MFA from Murray State University's low residency program in 2009. She has poems forthcoming in *The Hamilton Stone Review* and *Scapegoat Review*.

Anthony Rintala, *Southern Indiana Review*'s Media Editor, trained to write, edit, and teach poetry at the University of Southern Mississippi and Louisiana State University. Before coming to the University of Southern Indiana, he taught at LSU, Texas A&M University, Blinn Community College, and Ivy Tech College, and has edited for *Callaloo, New Delta Review, New Tex[t],* and *Blinn Literary Journal.* His poetry has most recently been published in *Kudzu Magazine, Muse: A Quarterly Journal, Ishaan Literary Review, Oklahoma Review, Copperfield Review, A Few Lines Magazine, Mad Hatter's Review, Foundling Review, Muddy River, Penwood Review,* and *St. Ann's Review.*

Daniel Romo is the author of *Romancing Gravity* (*Silver Birch Press,* 2013) and *When Kerosene's Involved* (*Black Coffee Press,* 2013). His poetry can be found in *The Los Angeles Review, Gargoyle, MiPOesias, Hobart,* and elsewhere. He holds an MFA from Queens University of Charlotte, and teaches English and creative writing. He accepts and rejects prose poems as the Guest Poetry Editor for Cease, Cows. He lives in Long Beach, CA and at www. danielromo.net.

Meeah Williams is a freelance writer and graphic artist. Her short fiction and poetry has most recently appeared or is forthcoming in *S(tick), Milo Review, Per Contra,* and *Vagabond City,* among others. She lives in Brooklyn, NY.

Lindsay Wilson, an English professor in Reno, Nevada, edits the literary journal, *The Meadow.* He has published four chapbooks, and his poetry has appeared in *The Minnesota Review, Verse Daily, The Portland Review, Salamander, The South Dakota Review,* as well as others.

FICTION

Nick Bertelson farms and writes in Iowa. His work has appeared in *The Coe Review, The Raleigh Review, Bull Magazine,* and others. He's currently working on a collection of short stories.

William Peskett was educated in Belfast and at Cambridge University, where he read natural sciences. He has worked in teaching, journalism, marketing, design management and corporate relations. He now lives and writes in Pattaya, Thailand. Peskett has published two volumes of poems, *The Nightowl's Dissection* and *Survivors,* the first of which won an Eric Gregory Award. These were followed by three novels, two collections of short stories, verse, and a volume of essays about ex-pat life in his adopted country. You can find more, contact the author and follow his blog on his website at www.williampeskett.com.

Jeremy Schnee received his MFA from Colorado State University. His short stories have appeared in *Chamber Four, The Cottonwood Review,* and *303 Magazine.* He works for a flour mill and has almost completed writing his first novel. For more about Jeremy's fiction, visit www.jeremyschnee.com.

Wendy C. Williford is a native Texan who began writing stories as early as the 5th grade. By the time she was 17, she had written her first unpublished novel and a broad collection of poems. Since then, she has written dozens of short stories, poems, stories for friends and family and a screenplay. She received a BA in History with a minor in Creative Writing from Stephen F. Austin State University in 2007. Currently, she is working on a novel set during the Scottish War for Independence. She also blogs about her experiences as a newly published writer at www.paperbackwriter28.net/

VISUAL ART

Brian Forrest is an artist born in Canada and bred in the US. His expressive drawing and painting style creates emotion on canvas.

Kendell James is an Oklahoma City based photographer. His love of photography began with the gift of a camera for his 11th Christmas and he has been photographing everything from family photos to landscapes ever since. Kendell is a photographer with the Oklahoma Army National Guard, as well as an accomplished musician and history buff. He pursues finding interesting destinations for photo expeditions in his spare time. He has compiled a huge variety of images including portraits, florals, landscapes, industrial and military photos. He currently lives in Mustang, Oklahoma with his wife, Donna. They have a daughter, Rhiannon, who attends University of Central Oklahoma and two dogs: Krizzo and Rusty.

Rhiannon James is an Oklahoma based freelance artist and a student at The University of Central Oklahoma. She mainly produces high-contrast portraits and videogame concept artwork.

Vinoth Rajendran is a self-taught artist working in the gaming industry as a concept artist in India. Drawing creatures has been his pastime ever since he can remember. Old school black and white artists have been a great inspiration to me. My works can be found online here http://gfxengine.blogspot.in.

Adam Roberts is a background / concept artist and illustrator based in London, UK. He recently graduated in Animation Production, having previously worked in China on animation projects, and is currently working as a freelance illustrator.

NONFICTION

Paul Buchanan lives in Southern California and enjoys writing fiction and literary journalism. His work has appeared in a number of literary journals, including *Marlboro Review, Storyquarterly, Cicada* and *Portland Review*.

Francis DiClemente lives in Syracuse, New York, where he works as a video producer. He is the author of three poetry chapbooks, *In Pursuit of Infinity* (Finishing Line Press, 2013), *Vestiges* (Alabaster Leaves Publishing, 2012) and *Outskirts of Intimacy* (Flutter Press, 2010). His blog can be found at www.francisdiclemente.wordpress.com.

Corey Ginsberg's writing has most recently appeared in such publications as *Third Coast, The Los Angeles Review, PANK, the cream city review, Puerto del Sol,* and *Subtropics,* among others. Corey currently lives in Miami and works as a freelance writer.

Melissa Grunow is an MFA student in creative nonfiction at National University. Her writing has appeared or is forthcoming in *The Quotable, The Adroit Journal, 94 Creations Literary Journal, Eunoia Review, Wilderness House Literary Review,* and others. She teaches English and creative writing courses at a small college in Michigan, and is writing her first book titled River City, a collection of essays. Visit her website at www.melissagrunow.com/.

Lockie Hunter is from a town in Appalachia where oral storytelling is vital to the community. She writes to safeguard the idiomatic expressions that are fast disappearing due to gentrification of the area. She holds an MFA in fiction from Emerson College in Boston and teaches creative writing at Warren Wilson College. Her words have appeared in publications including *Brevity, The Baltimore Review, Main Street Rag, Arts & Opinion, The Christian Science Monitor, Quarter After Eight, The Smart Set from Drexel University, Nerve.com* and others, and her poetry and flash fiction have been anthologized. You may find her words at www.lockiehunter.com.